Contents

Cover photograph by Paul Williams

Published by Hamlyn Publishing,
a division of The Hamlyn Publishing Group Limited,
Bridge House, London Road, Twickenham, Middlesex, England

© Copyright The Hamlyn Publishing Group Limited
1963, 1969
Tenth impression 1985

ISBN 0 600 32298 X

Printed and bound in Great Britain by R. J. Acford

D1364554

Some Useful Facts and Figures

Notes on metrication

In case you wish to convert quantities into metric measures, the following tables give a comparison.

Solid measures

Ounces	Approx. grams to nearest whole figure	Recommended conversion to nearest unit of 25
1	28	25
2	57	50
3	85	75
4	113	100
5	142	150
6	170	175
7	198	200
8	227	225
9	255	250
10	283	275
11	312	300
12	340	350
13	368	375
14	396	400
15	425	425
16 (1 lb)	454	450
17	482	475
18	510	500
19	539	550
20 (1¼ lb)	567	575

Note: When converting quantities over 20 oz first add the appropriate figures in the centre column, then adjust to the nearest unit of 25. As a general guide, 1 kg (1000 g) equals 2·2 lb or about 2 lb 3 oz. This method of conversion gives good results in nearly all cases, although in certain pastry and cake recipes a more accurate conversion is necessary to produce a balanced recipe.

Liquid measures

Imperial	Approx. millilitres to nearest whole figure	Recommended millilitres
¼ pint	142	150
½ pint	283	300
¾ pint	425	450
1 pint	567	600
1½ pints	851	900
1¾ pints	992	1000 (1 litre)

Oven temperatures

The table below gives recommended equivalents.

	°C	°F	Gas Mark
Very cool	110	225	¼
	120	250	½
Cool	140	275	1
	150	300	2
Moderate	160	325	3
	180	350	4
Moderately hot	190	375	5
	200	400	6
Hot	220	425	7
	230	450	8
Very hot	240	475	9

Notes for American and Australian users

In America the 8-oz measuring cup is used. In Australia metric measures are now used in conjunction with the standard 250-ml measuring cup. The Imperial pint, used in Britain and Australia, is 20 fl oz, while the American pint is 16 fl oz. It is important to remember that the Australian tablespoon differs from both the British and American tablespoons. The British standard tablespoon, which has been used throughout this book, holds 17·7 ml, the American 14·2 ml, and the Australian 20 ml. A teaspoon holds approximately 5 ml in all three countries.

Introduction

A dark rich cake, fragrant with spice and bursting with fruit, melt-in-the-mouth shortcake crowned with cream and studded with strawberries, multi-coloured fruits glistening in a golden pastry case . . . there is a cake for every occasion. In this book you will find all the recipes you require. If it gives you pleasure to serve a home-made cake with a really professional finish, read these tips, then choose your recipe. You will be surprised at how easy it is.

General Hints on Cake-making and Oven Temperatures

Flour in these recipes means PLAIN flour, unless otherwise stated. Use castor sugar, also, unless otherwise stated. Demerara, Barbados or soft brown sugar is used in making gingerbread and dark rich fruit cake. Granulated sugar may cause 'spotting'.

Butter or a soft or superfine margarine should be used for cake-making, although new methods can be used which call for whipped-up fats or oil. Cakes which are to be kept and matured should always be made with butter, and pastry should be made with firm, hard margarine, lard or other vegetable fats.

Eggs: Break each egg separately into a saucer before putting into the basin. Whisk slightly with a fork to mix the yolk and white.

Consistency of cake mixtures

Stiff dough: use as little liquid as possible, only sufficient to bind ingredients into a lump. Use for making biscuits and pastry.

Soft dough: add as much liquid as the mixture will take, without becoming so soft that it cannot be rolled out. Use for making yeast and scone doughs.

Stiff consistency or mixture: add enough liquid to make a mixture that is too sticky to handle or roll out—but which will keep its shape when dropped from a spoon, e.g. rock cakes.

Soft consistency or mixture: a mixture which will drop from the spoon in lumps, but is too thick to pour. Used for most cakes.

Pouring mixture: consistency of thick cream, spreads slowly when dropped from a spoon, e.g. dropped scones.

Preparing tins

An unsalted fat, e.g. lard or oil, should be used for brushing or greasing tins and lining paper. Cakes which require long, slow cooking should be lined with double greaseproof paper. A double strip of brown paper fastened round the outside of the tin will prevent the outside of the cake from being overcooked. A pad of newspaper on the shelf under the cake tin will protect the bottom of the cake which requires long, slow cooking.

Lining tins

To line a large tin: Cut a round or square of paper the same size as the base of the tin. Cut a strip long enough to go right round, and about $1\frac{1}{2}$ inches higher than the side of the tin. Make a fold about 1 inch deep along the bottom edge of the strip, snip with scissors at $\frac{1}{4}$-inch intervals. Put this strip into the tin, cut side down, so that the snipped portion lies flat on the bottom of the tin. Then press the base paper into position.

To line a Swiss roll tin: Cut a piece of paper 2 inches larger all round than the tin. Place the tin in the centre of the paper and make a cut from each corner of the paper as far as the corner of the tin. Grease tin, place paper inside, see that it fits closely and that the corner pieces overlap. Grease the inside of the paper.

5

To line a sandwich or sponge cake tin: Grease the tin lightly and place a round of greased greaseproof paper in the bottom of the tin. If liked, instead of lining with paper the greased tin may be dusted with a mixture of equal quantities of flour and castor sugar. Remember, if you use paper for lining, that it is the greased side of the paper that touches the mixture.

Oven temperatures

Set the thermostat to the number or temperature required. Switch on the electricity or light the gas, allowing 10–15 minutes for the oven to reach the required temperature before the cake is put in.

Arrange the shelves before heating the oven.

Small plain cakes, scones and Swiss rolls go near the top of the oven. Small rich cakes, sandwich and sponge cakes go just above the centre.

Larger cakes go in the centre, and very large rich cakes and shortbreads towards the bottom.

To make sure the cake is cooked, press it gently with a finger.

It should feel firm and resilient and should spring back when the finger is removed. The most reliable check is to hold the tin to your ear. If the cake is 'singing', or sizzling, return it to the oven for a few minutes until it is silent. Two minutes in the oven can make all the difference.

Storing cakes

Cakes should be stored in tightly closed tins and kept in a cool place. Do not attempt to store glacé iced or filled cakes or biscuits. To store a rich fruit cake, make the cake at least 6–8 weeks before it is required, to allow it to mature. Wrap in a double layer of greaseproof paper and seal with cellulose tape, or wrap in aluminium foil.

A fully iced cake should be similarly wrapped and stored in an airtight tin in a cool and dry place. Look at the cake periodically to make sure that it is keeping satisfactorily.

DESCRIPTION OF OVEN	APPROXIMATE TEMPERATURE CENTRE OF OVEN °F.	THERMOSTAT SETTING
Very Slow or Very Cool	200–250 250–300	$\frac{1}{4}$ = 240 $\frac{1}{2}$ = 265 1 = 290
Slow or Cool or Very Moderate	300–350	2 = 310 3 = 335
Moderate	350–375	4 = 350
Moderately Hot to Hot	375–400	5 = 375 6 = 400
Hot to Very Hot	425–450	7 = 425
Very Hot	450–500	8 = 450 9 = 470

Scones and Small Cakes

If you hope that your cakes and scones will earn you the reputation of being a good cook, there are two basic methods of mixing the ingredients to be learnt.

Rubbing in: in this method, the fat is rubbed into the flour by hand. The tips of the fingers are used to crumble the fat into very small pieces, and in the process the fat becomes coated with flour so that it finally looks like breadcrumbs. This method, which is used for plain mixtures, is also used for making short-crust pastry.

Creaming: in this method, the fat is beaten with a wooden spoon until soft, the sugar is then added, and the fat and sugar are beaten together until light in colour and fluffy. The flour is then folded in—a large metal spoon should be used for this, and care should be taken to ensure that the air which has been worked into the mixture by the creaming process is not 'knocked out'. This method is used for making rich mixtures.

Scones

cooking time   small scones 7–10 minutes; scone round 10–15 minutes

you will need:

8 oz. flour	1 oz. sugar
2 teaspoons baking powder	½ teaspoon salt
¼ pint milk	beaten egg or milk for
2 oz. fat (butter, margarine or lard)	glazing

1 Grease and flour a baking tray.
2 Sieve flour, baking powder and salt.
3 Rub fat into the flour with the fingertips.
4 Add the sugar and any other ingredients to be used (see following recipes).
5 Stir in the milk and mix quickly to a soft dough.
6 Turn out on to a floured surface. Flour hands and form dough into a ball. Cut into two pieces.
7 Press each lightly by hand, or roll, into a round, ¾-inch thick.
8 Cut out with a 2-inch cutter or divide each round into quarters with a sharp knife. Do not cut through.
9 Place on baking tray, brush with beaten egg or milk.
10 Bake in a hot oven 425°F.—Mark 7.
11 Cool on a wire tray. Serve hot or cold.

Breakfast scones

Use basic recipe with or without the sugar. Serve buttered with cherry jam or marmalade.

Brown scones

Make as for basic recipe, using half wholemeal and half white flour.

Cheese scones

Make as for basic recipe, omitting the sugar and adding 4 oz. grated cheese and a pinch of dry mustard.

Fancy scones

Make as for basic recipe, adding 1 oz. chopped mixed peel and 1 oz. chopped glacé cherries.

Fruit scones

Make as for basic recipe, adding 2 oz. currants, sultanas or raisins.

Ginger scones

Make as for basic recipe, omitting baking powder. Add ½ teaspoon bicarbonate of soda, ½ teaspoon powdered ginger and 1–2 tablespoons syrup or treacle.

Oatmeal scones

Make as for basic recipe, using 4 oz. flour and 4 oz. fine oatmeal.

Potato scones

Make as for basic recipe, using 4 oz. flour and 4 oz. cooked sieved potato.

Soda scones

Make as for basic recipe, omitting baking powder. Add 1 teaspoon cream of tartar and ½ teaspoon bicarbonate of soda.

Sour milk scones

Make as for basic recipe, omitting baking powder. Add ½ teaspoon bicarbonate of soda, ½ teaspoon cream of tartar and mix with ¼ pint sour milk.

Tea scones

Add 1 beaten egg to the basic recipe and use a little less milk. Serve hot with butter or cream and strawberry or raspberry jam.

Girdle scones

Use basic recipe. Divide each large piece of dough into 8 sections. Heat a girdle, the hot plate of an electric cooker, the girdle sheet of a cooker or frying pan, until moderately hot. Grease well. Cook scones for 4–5 minutes on each side. Serve hot.

Treacle scones

Make as ginger scones, omitting ginger and adding ½ teaspoon mixed spice.

Drop scones or Scotch pancakes

cooking time   6 minutes

Use basic scone recipe, adding 1 egg and increasing the milk to ½ pint.
1 Beat the liquid into the dry ingredients to make a thick batter.
2 Drop the mixture in small spoonfuls on to a moderately hot girdle, well greased.
3 When bubbles rise to the surface and the underside is lightly browned (3–4 minutes), turn scones over with a palette knife. Cook gently until cooked through.
4 Place at once in a clean tea-towel to keep moist. Serve hot with butter, honey or syrup.

Small plain cakes or buns

cooking time   15–20 minutes

you will need:

8 oz. flour	2 eggs
4 oz. margarine	2 teaspoons baking
4 oz. sugar	powder
3–4 oz. fruit (optional)	½ teaspoon salt
¼ teaspoon mixed spice	milk to mix
(optional)	

1 Grease patty tins, or use small paper cases.
2 Sieve flour, salt and baking powder into a bowl, with the spice, if used.
3 Rub in fat, until the mixture resembles breadcrumbs.
4 Add sugar and fruit, if used.
5 Beat the eggs and stir into the mixture, adding a little milk, if necessary, to mix to a dropping consistency.
6 Bake at 400°F.—Mark 6 for 5 minutes, then reduce heat to 350°F.—Mark 4 and cook until well risen and golden.

Cherry cakes

Make as above, adding 2 oz. glacé cherries and ½ teaspoon vanilla essence.

Chocolate cakes

Make as above, replacing 1 tablespoon flour with 1 tablespoon cocoa and adding ½ teaspoon vanilla essence.

Coconut buns

Make as above, adding 2 tablespoons coconut and ½ teaspoon vanilla essence.

Coffee buns

Make as before, adding 2 tablespoons coffee essence and 2 oz. currants.

Cinnamon buns

Make as before, adding ½ teaspoon cinnamon and ½ teaspoon grated lemon rind.

Ginger cakes

Make as before, adding 1 tablespoon treacle, ½ teaspoon bicarbonate of soda and ½ teaspoon ground ginger.

Ginger buns

Make as before, adding 2 oz. chopped ginger and ½ teaspoon ground ginger.

Rice buns

Make as before, replacing 2 oz. of the flour with 2 oz. ground rice.

Fruit buns

Make as before, adding 3–4 oz. raisins, currants or sultanas, 1 oz. chopped peel and ¼ teaspoon nutmeg.

Treacle buns

Make as before, omitting the baking powder and using ½ teaspoon bicarbonate of soda. Add 1 tablespoon treacle.

Raspberry buns

cooking time   15–20 minutes

you will need:

8 oz. self-raising flour	4 oz. sugar
pinch salt	milk to mix
3 oz. margarine	raspberry jam

1 Sieve flour and salt into a bowl.
2 Rub in fat until the mixture resembles breadcrumbs.
3 Stir in sugar.
4 Mix to a firm dough with a little milk.
5 Turn on to a lightly floured surface and knead lightly.
6 Divide into about 12 even-sized balls.
7 Make a hole in the centre of each by pressing with the thumb.
8 Fill holes with a small teaspoon raspberry jam.
9 Place on a greased baking tray. Bake on the middle shelf of a hot oven 400°F.—Mark 6.

Rock cakes

cooking time   10–15 minutes

you will need:

8 oz. self-raising flour	3 oz. mixed dried fruit
¼ teaspoon salt	1 egg
½ teaspoon mixed spice	2–3 teaspoons milk
3 oz. margarine	(depending on the size
3 oz. sugar	of the egg)

1 Sieve the flour, salt and spice into a bowl.
2 Rub in fat, until the mixture resembles bread-crumbs.
3 Stir in sugar and fruit.
4 Make a well in the centre of the mixture, pour in the egg, lightly beaten.
5 Mix to a stiff paste, using a fork, and adding milk.
6 Put spoonfuls of the mixture in rocky heaps on a greased baking sheet and bake in a hot oven 400°F.—Mark 6, on the middle shelf.

Raisin cakes

cooking time	20 minutes

you will need:

8 oz. self-raising flour	4 oz. sugar
½ teaspoon salt	1 egg
3 oz. margarine	milk to mix
4 oz. raisins, roughly chopped	

1 Sieve flour and salt into a bowl.
2 Rub in fat, until the mixture resembles bread-crumbs.
3 Add sugar and raisins.
4 Stir in egg, lightly beaten, and enough milk to give a soft dropping consistency.
5 Half fill paper baking cases on a baking tray.
6 Bake in a hot oven 400°F.—Mark 6 until golden.

Small rich cakes

cooking time	15–20 minutes

you will need:

8 oz. flour	2–4 eggs
6 oz. butter or margarine	1 teaspoon baking powder
6 oz. sugar	milk to mix
vanilla essence (optional)	½ teaspoon mixed spice
4–6 oz. fruit (optional)	(optional)

1 Prepare tins or paper baking cases.
2 Sieve the flour, baking powder and spice.
3 Beat the fat with a wooden spoon until soft.
4 Add the sugar and continue beating until the mixture becomes light and creamy. Add essence, if used.
5 Beat the eggs. Add a little at a time to the creamed mixture, beating well.
6 Lightly fold in the flour, using a metal spoon.
7 Lightly mix in the fruit, if used, adding a little milk, if necessary, to make a soft dropping consistency.
8 Spoon the mixture into the tins or paper cases until two-thirds full.
9 Bake in a moderately hot oven 375°F.—Mark 5 for 5 minutes, reduce the heat to 350°F.—Mark 4 and cook until golden.

10 Remove from oven, allow to cool for 5 minutes, then place on a wire tray until cold.

Coconut cakes

Make as before, spread tops of cakes with warm raspberry jam and sprinkle with coco-nut.

Walnut cakes

Make as before, adding ½ teaspoon vanilla essence and 2 oz. finely chopped walnuts.

Almond cakes

Make as before, adding ½ teaspoon almond essence. Spread tops of cakes with warm apricot jam and sprinkle each with chopped blanched almonds.

Seed cakes

Make as before, adding 2 teaspoons caraway seeds and 2 oz. mixed peel.

Chocolate chip cakes

Make as before, adding ½ teaspoon vanilla essence and 3–4 oz. plain chocolate, roughly chopped.

Cinnamon buns

cooking time	15–20 minutes

you will need:

1 lb. self-raising flour	6 oz. sugar
1 teaspoon powdered cinnamon	2 eggs
pinch salt	milk
6 oz. margarine	extra sugar and cinnamon

1 Grease a baking tray.
2 Sieve flour, cinnamon and salt.
3 Rub in fat, until the mixture resembles bread-crumbs.
4 Stir in sugar.
5 Stir in the eggs, saving a little, and add enough milk to make a stiff dough.
6 Mix thoroughly, divide into sixteen portions and place on a greased baking tray.
7 Mix remaining egg with a little milk and brush over each bun.
8 Dust each with a mixture of sugar and cin-namon.
9 Bake in a moderate oven 350°F.—Mark 4.

Queen cakes

cooking time 20 minutes

you will need:

6 oz. self-raising flour
good pinch salt
4 oz. butter or margarine
4 oz. castor sugar

2 eggs
milk to mix
4 oz. currants

1 Sieve flour and salt into a bowl.
2 Cream fat and sugar until light and fluffy.
3 Beat eggs lightly with a fork, beat into the creamed fat, folding in a little flour.
4 Stir in the milk. Fold in the remaining flour, using a metal spoon, and stir in the fruit.
5 Half fill paper baking cases (about 20) on a baking sheet, or greased patty tins.
6 Bake on the middle shelf of a moderately hot oven 375°F.—Mark 5.
The flavour may be varied by adding 2–3 drops of vanilla essence, grated lemon or orange rind to the creamed fat.

Almond twists

cooking time 10 minutes

you will need:

5 oz. flour
pinch salt
3 oz. butter
2 dessertspoons castor
    sugar
1 egg

few drops almond essence
topping:
little beaten egg white
castor sugar
chopped almonds
    (optional)

1 Sift flour with salt.
2 Rub fat in lightly, until mixture resembles breadcrumbs.
3 Add the sugar.
4 Stir in beaten egg and essence. Mix to a soft dough.
5 Divide dough into nine equal portions; on a lightly-floured surface, roll each into a 'sausage', about 7 inches long.
6 Curl each round into a 'pincurl' shape. Place on a baking sheet.
7 Brush the top of each with egg white, and sprinkle with castor sugar and finely chopped blanched almonds, if available.
8 Bake in a hot oven 400°F.—Mark 6 until golden.
9 Leave to cool on a wire tray.

Chocolate cakes

cooking time 15–20 minutes

you will need:

5 oz. self-raising flour
1 oz. cocoa
good pinch salt
3 oz. butter or margarine
3 oz. sugar

2 eggs
3–4 drops vanilla essence
milk to mix
chocolate glacé icing (see
    page 35)

1 Sieve flour, cocoa and salt into a bowl.
2 Cream fat and sugar. Add the essence.
3 Beat in eggs, folding in a little flour.
4 Fold in remaining flour and lightly stir in the milk.
5 Three-quarters fill paper baking cases (12–15) on a baking sheet.
6 Bake on the middle shelf of a moderately hot oven 375°F.—Mark 5.
7 Cool on a wire tray. When cold, top each with a teaspoon of chocolate glacé icing.

Mushroom cakes

Make cakes as above. Cut out centres with a small sharp-pointed knife or apple corer, not quite through to the bottom. Fill the centre with some butter cream (see page 33) and replace the top. Dust with icing sugar.

Butterfly cakes

Make cakes as above. When cool, cut off tops. Make a small hollow in the centre of each with a teaspoon. Place a good teaspoon lemon butter cream (see page 33) in the centre of each. Cut the tops in half and replace, rounded edges, outwards, to resemble wings. Dust with icing sugar.

Apricot surprise cakes

Make cakes as above. When cool, cut off tops and make a small hollow in each. Fill with a teaspoon apricot jam and a little chopped almond, if liked. Replace top.

Madeleines

cooking time 20 minutes

you will need:

4 oz. flour
4 oz. butter
4 oz. sugar
2 eggs

raspberry jam
desiccated coconut
glacé cherries

1 Grease twelve dariole tins and place on a baking sheet.
2 Sieve flour.
3 Cream fat and sugar.
4 Beat in eggs, adding a little flour.
5 Fold in remaining flour.
6 Three-quarters fill each tin with mixture.
7 Bake at 375°F.—Mark 5 until risen and brown.
8 Turn out on to a wire tray and leave until cold.
9 Trim cakes so that they are even in size and level at the bottom.

10 Sieve jam and heat gently. Brush over each cake.

11 Roll each cake in desiccated coconut, which has been sprinkled thickly on a sheet of paper or foil.

12 Dip a cherry in the jam and stick on the top of each madeleine.

Golden cakes

cooking time   15–20 minutes

you will need:

8 oz. flour	3 eggs
½ teaspoon baking powder	3 tablespoons marmalade
4 oz. margarine	pinch salt
4 oz. sugar	lemon icing

1 Grease eighteen queen cake or deep patty tins.
2 Sieve flour, baking powder and salt.
3 Cream fat and sugar.
4 Beat in the eggs one at a time, beating each in well before adding the next.
5 Stir in the marmalade.
6 Fold in the dry ingredients.
7 Half fill prepared tins.
8 Bake at 375°F.—Mark 5.
9 Cool on a wire tray. Top each with lemon glacé icing (see page 35).

Swiss tarts

cooking time   30 minutes

you will need:

4 oz. flour	2–3 drops vanilla essence
4 oz. butter or margarine	icing sugar
1 oz. castor sugar	raspberry jam or glacé cherries

1 Sieve the flour.
2 Cream the fat and sugar until light and fluffy, adding the vanilla essence.
3 Fold in the sieved flour.
4 Using a forcing bag and a large star nozzle, pipe the mixture into paper cases on a baking sheet. Start at the centre of the bottom of each case and pipe with a spiral movement round the sides, leaving a shallow depression in the centre.
5 Bake at 375°F.—Mark 5. Cool on a wire tray.
6 When tarts are cold, dust with icing sugar and fill centre with a teaspoon jam or a halved glacé cherry.

Feather cakes

cooking time   12–15 minutes

you will need:

5 oz. self-raising flour	2 eggs
3 oz. butter	1 tablespoon cream
3 oz. sugar	icing sugar

1 Grease twelve patty tins and dust with a little flour.
2 Sieve the flour.
3 Cream the butter and sugar, and beat in the eggs.
4 Fold in the flour and cream.
5 Spoon into the tins and bake in a moderately hot oven 375°F.—Mark 5.
6 Cool on a wire tray and dust with icing sugar.

Lemon feather cakes

Make as above. When cold, cut the top off each cake. Make a small hollow with a teaspoon. Fill with lemon curd, replace the top and coat with glacé icing (see page 34).

Honey feather cakes

Make as above, using only 1 oz. sugar. Add 2 oz. honey and a pinch mixed spice.

Coconut feather cakes

Make as above, replacing 1 oz. flour with 1 oz. coconut. Top with a glacé cherry.

Brownies

Make as above. Sprinkle the top of each cake with grated chocolate as soon as they come out of the oven.

Sultana and ginger poppets

cooking time   20–25 minutes

you will need:

4 oz. sultanas	4 oz. margarine
2 oz. crystallised ginger	4 oz. castor sugar
2 oz. mixed peel	finely grated rind 1 orange
4 oz. self-raising flour	2 eggs

1 Grease twenty shallow bun or patty tins.
2 Mix sultanas with the peel and ginger, roughly chopped.
3 Place a little of the fruit into each tin.
4 Sieve flour.
5 Cream fat and sugar, adding orange rind.
6 Beat in the eggs.
7 Fold in the flour.
8 Place a good teaspoon of the mixture into each tin.
9 Bake on the second shelf from the top in a moderately hot oven, 375°F.—Mark 5.
10 Turn out carefully and cool upside-down on a wire tray.
11 When cold, coat cakes upside-down with plain or lemon flavoured glacé icing, as liked (see page 35).

Cherry and coconut poppets

Make as previous recipe, omitting sultanas and ginger, and using 4 oz. glacé cherries. When cakes are cold, brush tops with warmed apricot jam and sprinkle thickly with toasted coconut.

To prepare toasted coconut

Sprinkle coconut on to a clean, dry baking sheet. Place on the top shelf of a very moderate oven 335°F.—Mark 3 for 3–5 minutes. Run a fork through the coconut once or twice while it is in the oven.

Every Day Cakes

It's such a comfort to know that there is a home-made cake in the tin when a friend drops in for a cup of tea, and what satisfaction to be able to say: 'Yes, I made it myself.'

Most large cakes are made by the rubbing in or creaming method, the exception being gingerbread, which is made by the melting method. For this method, the fat, sugar and treacle are warmed together before being stirred into the dry ingredients.

Gingerbread improves on keeping, and this is one cake that you needn't be ashamed to serve if it has sunk in the middle.

Every day cake

cooking time   1¼–1½ hours

you will need:

8 oz. self-raising flour	5 oz. sugar
4 oz. margarine	2 eggs
8 oz. dried fruit	5 tablespoons milk

1 Grease and line a 6-inch cake tin or a 2-lb. loaf tin.
2 Sieve the flour.
3 Rub in the margarine, add the fruit and sugar and mix well.
4 Beat the eggs with the milk and stir into the dry ingredients.
5 Turn into the prepared tin and bake in a moderate oven 350°F.—Mark 4.
6 Cool on a wire tray.

Family fruit cake (eggless)

cooking time   about 2 hours

you will need:

1 lb. flour	3 oz. glacé cherries, quartered
1 level teaspoon salt	
8 oz. castor sugar	4 oz. chopped mixed peel
6 oz. margarine	2 level teaspoons bicarbonate of soda
8 oz. currants	
6 oz. sultanas	½ pint milk
4 oz. seedless raisins	3 tablespoons malt vinegar

1 Grease an 8-inch round tin, place a round of greased greaseproof paper in the bottom.
2 Sieve flour and salt into a bowl and add the sugar.
3 Rub in fat until mixture resembles breadcrumbs.
4 Stir in fruit.
5 Dissolve the bicarbonate of soda in milk, add the vinegar.
6 Stir quickly into the dry ingredients, using a wooden spoon. Beat until well mixed and smooth.
7 Turn into the tin and smooth top with a palette knife.
8 Bake in the centre of a moderate oven 350°F. —Mark 4. Cover cake with a double sheet of greaseproof paper after the first hour to prevent over browning.
9 Turn out on to a wire tray to cool.

Madeira cake

cooking time   1–1¼ hours

you will need:

8 oz. flour	finely grated rind 1 lemon
pinch salt	3 eggs
1 teaspoon baking powder	milk to mix, about
5 oz. butter or margarine	3 tablespoons
5 oz. sugar	citron peel (optional)

1 Grease and line a 6-inch cake tin.
2 Sieve the flour, salt and baking powder.
3 Cream the fat and sugar, and add the lemon rind.
4 Gradually beat in the eggs.
5 Fold in the flour, adding the milk to give a soft dropping consistency.
6 Put into the prepared tin, bake in a moderate oven 350°F.—Mark 4.
7 If citron peel is used, cut into strips and carefully place 2 or 3 strips on the top of the cake after it has been in the oven for about 30 minutes.

Cherry cake

Wash 3 oz. glacé cherries in a sieve under the hot tap. Dry in a clean tea towel and cut into quarters. Make as for madeira cake, adding the cherries to the sieved flour. Omit the citron peel.

Almond cherry cake

cooking time   1½ hours

you will need:

6 oz. flour	6 oz. margarine
2 oz. ground almonds	6 oz. castor sugar
6 oz. cherries	3 eggs

1 Grease and line a 7-inch cake tin.
2 Sieve the flour and add the ground almonds.
3 Cut the cherries in half and mix with the flour.
4 Cream the fat and sugar, and beat in the eggs.
5 Fold in the flour mixture.
6 Turn into the prepared tin and bake at 335°F. —Mark 3.

Dundee cake (eggless)

cooking time   about 2 hours 45 minutes

you will need:

2 oz. glacé cherries	finely grated rind 1 orange
4 oz. blanched almonds	finely grated rind 2 lemons
½ pint water	1 large can full cream
10 oz. margarine	sweetened condensed
8 oz. sultanas	milk
8 oz. currants	10 oz. flour
4 oz. chopped mixed peel	¾ level teaspoon
pinch salt	bicarbonate of soda

1 Chop the cherries and 2 oz. of the almonds. Split remaining almonds in halves.
2 Put the water, margarine, all the fruit, the chopped almonds, grated rinds and condensed milk in a saucepan.
3 Bring to the boil, stirring all the time. Lower the heat and simmer for 3 minutes. Remove and cool.
4 Grease and line an 8-inch cake tin.
5 Sieve the flour and salt into a mixing bowl.
6 Stir bicarbonate of soda into the cooked fruit mixture.
7 Stir the fruit mixture quickly into the flour and mix well.
8 Turn into the tin, spread evenly. Arrange remaining almonds on top.
9 Bake in a slow oven 310°F.—Mark 2.
10 Turn on to a wire tray to cool.
    This is a 'rich tasting' moist cake, which keeps well. Half this mixture may be cooked in a 6-inch tin. Allow 2 hours cooking time.

Honey cake

cooking time   1 hour

you will need:

8 oz. self-raising flour	2 eggs
5 oz. margarine	4 tablespoons milk
2½ oz. sugar	pinch salt
3 oz. thick honey	grated rind 1 lemon

1 Grease and line a 7-inch cake tin.
2 Sieve the flour and salt.
3 Cream fat, sugar and honey, adding the lemon rind. Beat in the eggs.
4 Fold in the flour, alternately with the milk.
5 Turn into the prepared tin and bake at 350°F. —Mark 4.

Cherry cake

Make as above, adding 2 oz. chopped glacé cherries to the sieved flour.

Spice cake

Make as above, adding ½ teaspoon ground ginger or cinnamon to the flour before sieving.

Dundee cake

cooking time   3 hours

you will need:

2 oz. almonds	8 oz. castor sugar
2 oz. glacé cherries	grated rind ½ lemon
4 oz. candied peel	4 eggs
8 oz. currants	8 oz. flour
8 oz. sultanas	1 level teaspoon baking
2 oz. cornflour	powder
8 oz. butter	

1 Grease and line an 8-inch cake tin.
2 Blanch the almonds, chop 1 oz. and split the remainder in halves.
3 Wash and chop the cherries and peel. Clean the currants and sultanas, if necessary.
4 Put all the fruit and the chopped almonds in a bowl and coat well with the cornflour.
5 Cream the butter and sugar, adding the lemon rind.
6 Beat in the eggs, one at a time.
7 Sieve the flour and baking powder, fold into the creamed mixture.
8 Lightly stir in the fruit coated with cornflour.
9 Put the mixture into the prepared tin.
10 Bake in a slow oven 310°F.—Mark 2. Arrange the split almonds on the top of the cake after it has been in the oven for 30 minutes.

Orange cider cake

cooking time   45 minutes

you will need:

8 oz. flour	1 teaspoon mixed spice
2 teaspoons baking powder	grated rind 1 orange
4 oz. butter	8 oz. sultanas
6 oz. sugar	$\frac{1}{4}$ pint sweet cider
2 eggs	orange glacé icing (see
1 teaspoon cinnamon	page 35)

1 Grease and line a 7-inch cake tin.
2 Sieve the dry ingredients, adding the orange rind and sultanas.
3 Cream the fat and sugar.
4 Beat in the eggs, one at a time.
5 Lightly stir in the dry ingredients, using cider to make a dropping consistency.
6 Bake in a moderate oven 350°F.—Mark 4.
7 Allow to cool on a wire tray and, when cold, coat with orange glacé icing.

Date loaf

cooking time   about 1 hour

you will need:

10 oz. self-raising flour	2 tablespoons marmalade
$\frac{1}{4}$ teaspoon salt	6–8 oz. chopped dates
4 oz. margarine	1 teaspoon almond essence
4 oz. sugar	about $\frac{1}{4}$ pint milk
2 large eggs	

1 Grease and line a 2-lb. tin.
2 Sieve flour and salt.
3 Cream fat and sugar, add essence and gradually beat in eggs and marmalade.
4 Fold in the flour and salt.
5 Lightly stir in dates and milk to give a soft dropping consistency.
6 Bake in a moderate oven 350°F.—Mark 4.
7 Turn out on to a wire tray to cool.
8 Serve sliced and spread with butter.

Cherry loaf

cooking time   about 1 hour 10 minutes

you will need:

10 oz. flour	1 teaspoon vanilla essence
2 rounded teaspoons	1 egg
baking powder	1 small can condensed milk
6 oz. butter or margarine	8–10 tablespoons water
4 oz. glacé cherries,	
quartered	

1 Grease and line a loaf tin—1 to 1$\frac{1}{2}$-lb. size.
2 Sieve the flour and baking powder into a bowl.
3 Rub in the fat.
4 Add cherries, stir in egg and vanilla essence.
5 Stir in the milk and sufficient water to make a dropping consistency.
6 Bake in a moderate oven 350°F.—Mark 4.
7 Cool on a wire tray. Dust with icing sugar.

Orange loaf cake

cooking time   1$\frac{1}{4}$ hours

you will need:

8 oz. self-raising flour	grated rind 2 oranges
6 oz. butter	3 eggs
6 oz. sugar	milk

1 Grease and line a 1-lb. loaf tin.
2 Sieve the flour.
3 Cream the fat and sugar, adding the orange rind.
4 Beat in the eggs.
5 Fold in the flour, adding sufficient milk to give a soft dropping consistency.
6 Turn the mixture into the prepared tin and sprinkle the top with castor sugar.
7 Bake in a moderate oven 350°F.—Mark 4.
8 Leave on a wire tray to cool.

Old-fashioned cake

cooking time   1$\frac{3}{4}$ hours

you will need:

8 oz. self-raising flour	8 oz. raisins
1 rounded teaspoon mixed	8 oz. currants
spice	4 oz. sultanas
1 level teaspoon grated	4 oz. mixed peel
nutmeg	$\frac{1}{4}$ pint milk, plus
pinch salt	2 tablespoons
5 oz. margarine	2 eggs
6 level tablespoons golden	$\frac{1}{2}$ level teaspoon
syrup	bicarbonate of soda
4 oz. chopped, stoned dates	

1 Grease and line a 7-inch cake tin.
2 Sieve flour, spice and salt into a mixing bowl.
3 Gently heat syrup, margarine, fruit, peel and milk in a pan. When the margarine has melted, simmer gently for 5 minutes, stirring once or twice.
4 Remove and allow to cool slightly.
5 Make a well in the centre of the dry ingredients.
6 Add eggs, do not stir.
7 Add bicarbonate to syrup mixture and pour at once into the mixing bowl.
8 Beat all together thoroughly.
9 Pour into tin and bake on the middle shelf of a slow oven 310°F.—Mark 2.
10 Turn on to a wire tray to cool.

Farmhouse cake

cooking time   1$\frac{1}{4}$–1$\frac{1}{2}$ hours

you will need:

8 oz. self-raising flour	4–6 oz. mixed currants,
$\frac{1}{4}$ level teaspoon salt	sultanas and raisins
4 oz. margarine	2 eggs
4 oz. sugar	3 tablespoons milk
2 oz. halved glacé cherries	2 oz. chopped blanched
	almonds

1 Grease and line a 7-inch cake tin.
2 Sieve the flour and salt into a bowl.

3 Rub in the margarine and stir in the sugar, cherries and dried fruit.

4 Stir in the eggs and milk, and turn into the prepared tin. Sprinkle with chopped nuts.

5 Bake on the middle shelf of a moderate oven 350°F.—Mark 4.

6 Turn out, remove the paper and cool on a wire tray.

Australian fruit cake

cooking time   2½ hours

you will need:

8 oz. butter	8 oz. sultanas
4 oz. honey (2 tablespoons)	8 oz. raisins
6 oz. sugar	4 oz. glacé cherries
2 tablespoons boiling water	1 teaspoon cocoa
12 oz. self-raising flour	½ teaspoon mixed spice
2 oz. cornflour	½ teaspoon each vanilla
½ teaspoon salt	and almond essence
3 eggs	

1 Grease and line a 7-inch cake tin.

2 Put butter, honey, sugar and boiling water into a large bowl.

3 Cream until light and smooth, adding the essences.

4 Sieve the flours, cocoa, spice and salt.

5 Beat the eggs into the creamed mixture, adding about 1 dessertspoon of the flour.

6 Mix the fruit and flour together and stir lightly into the creamed mixture.

7 Turn into the prepared tin and bake at 310°F. —Mark 2.

8 Leave on a wire tray to cool.

If a shallow cake is preferred, bake the mixture in an 8-inch tin for 2 hours.

Chocolate cake

cooking time   30 minutes

you will need:

6 oz. flour	1 egg
pinch salt	2 oz. plain chocolate
1 level teaspoon baking powder	2 tablespoons milk
	chocolate icing (see page 35) or icing sugar
3 oz. butter or margarine	
2½ oz. sugar	

1 Grease and line a 7-inch tin.

2 Sieve flour, salt and baking powder.

3 Cream the fat and sugar, and beat in the egg.

4 Chop the chocolate and place with the milk in a basin, over a small pan of hot water.

5 Heat gently until the chocolate melts. Allow to cool.

6 Beat the chocolate into the fat and sugar.

7 Lightly fold in the sieved ingredients and pour into the prepared tin.

8 Bake in a moderately hot oven 375°F.—Mark 5.

9 Cool on a wire tray. Coat with icing or sprinkle with icing sugar.

Rich chocolate cake

cooking time   45–50 minutes

you will need:

3 oz. plain chocolate	4 oz. butter
8 level tablespoons honey	3 oz. castor sugar
6 oz. plain flour	1 teaspoon vanilla essence
1 level teaspoon bicarbonate of soda	2 eggs
¾ teaspoon salt	scant ¼ pint water

1 Grease and line the bases of two 8-inch sandwich tins.

2 Place chocolate and honey in small basin over pan of hot water. Stir until chocolate has melted, beat well and leave to cool.

3 Sieve flour, bicarbonate of soda and salt together three times.

4 Cream butter, beat in sugar and continue beating until light and fluffy.

5 Beat in chocolate mixture, then eggs one at a time. Add vanilla essence.

6 Stir in flour, a little at a time, alternately with water.

7 Beat well and pour mixture into tins.

8 Bake in a moderate oven, 350°F.—Mark 4. Cool slightly before turning out of tins.

Honey chocolate icing

you will need:

6 oz. plain chocolate	2 tablespoons warm water
4 level tablespoons honey	8 oz. icing sugar

To make icing, place chocolate and honey in small basin over pan of hot water. Stir until chocolate has melted—remove from pan and allow to cool slightly. Beat in half the sugar, stir in water and remaining sugar and beat well. Spread one cake with icing and place second cake on top. Coat top and sides of cake with icing, roughing up with knife into swirls.

Honey nut bread

cooking time   1½ hours

you will need:

4 oz. margarine	3 level teaspoons baking powder
4 oz. castor sugar	
6 level tablespoons honey	1 level teaspoon salt
1 egg	¼ pint milk (good measure)
10½ oz. plain flour	4 oz. chopped walnuts

1 Grease a 2-lb. loaf tin.

2 Cream margarine and sugar, mix in honey thoroughly. Beat in egg.

3 Sieve flour, baking powder and salt, and stir into creamed mixture alternately with milk. Mix in nuts.

4 Spread mixture into tin.

5 Bake in a moderate oven 350°F.—Mark 4, cool on a wire tray.

Mallow spice cake

cooking time   45 minutes

you will need:

6 oz. self-raising flour	3 oz. soft brown sugar
½ level teaspoon salt	3 oz. butter or margarine
2 rounded teaspoons mixed spice	2 eggs
	3 tablespoons milk

1 Grease a 1-lb. loaf tin.
2 Sieve the dry ingredients together. Add the sugar and rub in the fat.
3 Mix to a soft dropping consistency with the eggs and milk, stirring briskly, but without beating.
4 Turn into the prepared tin and bake in the centre of a moderate oven 350°F.—Mark 4.
5 When cold, cut into 3 layers.
6 Fill and frost the cake with marshmallow frosting and leave in a cool place until firm.
7 Decorate with slices of preserved ginger, if liked.

Marshmallow frosting

you will need:

4 oz. pink and white marshmallows	2 egg whites
2 tablespoons milk	1 oz. sugar

1 Melt the marshmallows slowly in the milk and leave to cool, stirring occasionally.
2 Beat the egg whites and sugar until stiff and standing in peaks.
3 Fold in the marshmallow mixture and leave to set slightly before using.

Gingerbread

cooking time   50–60 minutes

you will need:

8 oz. flour	4 oz. soft brown sugar
3–4 level teaspoons ground ginger	4 oz. golden syrup
1 level teaspoon bicarbonate of soda	4 oz. black treacle
¼ pint milk	1 egg
4 oz. margarine	lemon glacé icing (see page 35), preserved ginger

1 Grease a square 7-inch tin and line the bottom with greased greaseproof paper.
2 Sieve flour and ginger into a mixing bowl.

3 Dissolve the bicarbonate of soda with 1 tablespoon of the milk.
4 Heat the remaining milk, fat, sugar, syrup and treacle gently until melted, stirring throughout.
5 Remove from the heat and leave until cool.
6 Stir the liquid into the flour, beat in the egg and continue beating until smooth.
7 Stir in the dissolved bicarbonate and put the mixture into the prepared tin.
8 Bake in a moderate oven 350°F.—Mark 4 on the middle shelf.
9 Leave in the tin for 5 minutes, then turn out on to a wire tray to cool.
10 When cold, coat with lemon glacé icing and decorate with slices of preserved ginger, if liked.

Gingerbread (quick method)

cooking time   20 minutes

you will need:

4 oz. plain flour	3 tablespoons oil
pinch salt	2 oz. demerara sugar
2 level teaspoons ground ginger	4 oz. syrup and black treacle mixed
½ level teaspoon bicarbonate of soda	1 egg
	3 tablespoons milk

1 Grease a shallow 7-inch square tin and line the bottom with greased greaseproof paper.
2 Sieve flour, salt, ginger and bicarbonate of soda into a bowl.
3 Add the remaining ingredients and beat well until smooth and glossy.
4 Pour into the prepared tin and bake at 375°F. —Mark 5 on the third shelf from the top.
5 Turn out on to a wire tray and leave until cold.
6 Serve sliced and buttered, or coat with glacé icing (see page 34) and decorate with slices of preserved ginger.
To make tea bread, use mixed spice instead of ginger. Raisins or sultanas, chopped mixed peel or chopped walnuts may be added to this mixture.

Yeast Cakes and Buns

The delicious smell of warm crusty bread, and shiny brown currant buns—cooking with yeast has an air of magic about it, but there is really no mystique.

You can be sure of good results if you follow the recipes carefully, and you'll discover a new branch of cookery that is most satisfying and rewarding. Next time you feel irritable, try kneading a yeast dough—it works wonders!

All recipes give fresh yeast, but dried may be used. 1 oz. fresh yeast is equal to ½ oz. or 1 level tablespoon dried yeast.

Sprinkle the dried yeast on to a cupful of liquid taken from the total amount given in the recipe. Add a teaspoon of sugar or honey. Leave in a warm place until frothy—about 10 minutes. Use with the remaining liquid as described in the method.

Plum bread

cooking time   2 hours

you will need:

12 oz. self-raising flour	2 oz. cherries
¼ teaspoon nutmeg	2 oz. mixed peel
4 oz. margarine	6 oz. sugar
3 oz. sultanas	1 oz. yeast
6 oz. currants	½ pint warm milk
3 oz. raisins	

1 Grease and line a 2-lb. loaf tin.
2 Sieve flour and nutmeg.
3 Rub in the margarine.
4 Add the fruit and all the sugar except 1 teaspoon.
5 Cream the yeast with the 1 teaspoon sugar until liquid.
6 Make a well in the centre of the dry ingredients, stir in the yeast and the warm milk gradually.
7 Stir until mixture has been absorbed and pour into the tin. Bake at 310°F.—Mark 2. Cover the top of the loaf with greaseproof paper after it has been in the oven for 1 hour.

Coconut tea-time loaf

cooking time   40–45 minutes

you will need:

1-lb. flour	½ pint warm milk and water mixed
1 level teaspoon salt	
3 oz. desiccated coconut	½ oz. fresh yeast
1 oz. sugar	1 level teaspoon sugar extra coconut

1 Grease two 1-lb. loaf tins. Sprinkle with a little extra coconut.
2 Stir the sugar and yeast into milk and water. Blend in 1 tablespoon of the flour. Leave in a warm place until frothy.
3 Put remaining flour, salt and 3 oz. coconut and the 1 oz. sugar into a large bowl.
4 Make a well in the centre and stir in the yeast liquid, making a soft dough. Knead well by pulling dough up and pressing down until it feels firm and elastic.
5 Place the dough in a large greased polythene bag (brush inside of bag with oil or melted butter). Leave in a warm place until the dough doubles its size, and springs back when touched—about 50–60 minutes.
6 Turn dough on to a board dusted lightly with flour and coconut. Knead lightly, divide in

two. Flatten each piece of dough with the knuckles and roll up like a Swiss roll.
7 Place in the tins and sprinkle coconut on top of each. Cover the tins with a greased polythene bag, or greaseproof paper. Put in a warm place until the bread rises to the top of the tin—about 30 minutes.
8 Bake on the middle shelf at 425°F.—Mark 7.
9 Serve with butter and raspberry or apricot jam, or honey.

Ring loaf

Make dough as above, half fill greased ring moulds, sprinkle tops thickly with coconut and bake as above.

Iced coconut loaf

Make as above. When loaf is cool, coat with a mixture of coconut and icing sugar blended with lemon juice.

Coconut rolls

Prepare the dough as above, divide into small pieces and form into small smooth balls. Roll each in coconut and place on a lightly greased and floured tray. Put to rise in a warm place. Bake towards the top of the oven at 425°F.—Mark 7.

Orange bread

cooking time   30–35 minutes

you will need:

1 lb. plain flour	1 oz. fresh yeast
1 level teaspoon salt	1 teaspoon honey
1 oz. sugar	1 egg
¼ pint warm water	1 orange, minced or finely chopped—about 6 oz.

1 Grease two 1-lb. loaf tins.
2 Stir the honey and yeast into the water. Leave in a warm place until frothy.
3 Sieve flour and salt, add the sugar.
4 Make a well in the centre of the flour, add the egg, lightly beaten, the orange and the yeast liquid. Mix to a soft dough and knead well until firm.
5 Place the dough in a well greased polythene bag. Put to rise in a warm place for 40–50 minutes.
6 Turn dough on to a floured surface and knead lightly for 1–2 minutes. Divide the dough into two pieces and shape into rolls to fit the tins.
7 Place the shaped dough in the tins, cover and leave in a warm place to rise again for 30–40 minutes.
8 Bake on the middle shelf at 400°F.—Mark 6.
9 Turn the bread on to a wire tray, brush the top of each with melted butter, if liked.

Bath buns

cooking time 20 minutes

you will need:

1 lb. flour	3 oz. sultanas
6 oz. butter	2 oz. chopped peel
1 oz. yeast	$\frac{1}{2}$ lemon
1 oz. sugar	5 oz. castor sugar
$\frac{1}{4}$ pint milk	egg or milk to glaze
2 eggs	crushed loaf sugar

1 Sieve the flour and leave in a warm place.
2 Grease a baking sheet.
3 Cream the yeast with 1 teaspoon sugar (taken from 1 oz.). Heat the milk until tepid and stir into the yeast.
4 Rub the fat into the flour and add the remaining sugar.
5 Make a well in the centre of the flour mixture, beat in the eggs and the yeast mixture.
6 Beat well, adding a little more milk if needed to make a soft dough.
7 Cover and leave to rise until double its size—about 1 hour.
8 Mix fruit, lemon rind (finely grated) and the 5 oz. sugar. Warm slightly.
9 Turn the dough out on to a floured surface and roughly mix in the fruit mixture.
10 Divide the dough into 12–14 buns, place on the sheet. Leave in a warm place for 10 minutes.
11 Brush with glaze, sprinkle with crushed sugar.
12 Bake at 450°F.—Mark 8—until golden.

Sally Lunn tea-cakes

cooking time 15–20 minutes

you will need:

12 oz. flour	1 egg, beaten
$\frac{1}{4}$ teaspoon salt	1 oz. lard or margarine,
$\frac{1}{2}$ oz. yeast	melted
1 teaspoon sugar	egg or milk, and sugar to
$\frac{1}{8}$ pint milk and water	glaze

1 Grease and flour four small round tins.
2 Sieve flour and salt into a bowl.
3 Cream the yeast and sugar, and heat the milk until just tepid. Stir into the yeast.
4 Make a well in the centre of the flour, quickly stir in the yeast liquid, egg and fat.
5 Mix to a soft dough and knead well. Divide into four pieces.
6 Shape into rounds and place in the tins. The tins should be half filled.
7 Leave in a warm place until dough rises to the top of the tins.
8 Bake in a very hot oven 450°F.—Mark 8. Brush with glaze during the last 5 minutes of cooking time. Cool on a wire tray. If liked, omit glaze and coat tea-cakes with glacé icing (see page 34) when cold.

Yorkshire tea-cakes

Make as before, adding 2 oz. currants or sultanas. Leave the dough to rise in the bowl, then knead and shape into cakes. Prove in a warm place for 10 minutes. Bake in a very hot oven 450°F.—Mark 8, for 15 minutes. Finish as for Sally Lunns.

Swiss buns

Make as for Sally Lunns, shaping mixture into finger-length rolls. Bake in a very hot oven 450°F.—Mark 8, for about 20 minutes. When cold, coat with white glacé icing (see page 34).

Hot cross buns

cooking time 15–20 minutes

you will need:

1 lb. plain flour	3 oz. currants
pinch salt	1 oz. candied peel
$\frac{1}{2}$ pint milk and water	1 level teaspoon cinnamon
$\frac{1}{2}$ oz. yeast	1 level teaspoon nutmeg
2 oz. castor sugar	1 egg
2 oz. butter	shortcrust pastry (using 2 oz. flour)

1 Sieve half the flour into a mixing bowl.
2 Cream the yeast with 1 teaspoon of the sugar and stir in the lukewarm milk and water.
3 Pour into the sieved flour and mix well together.
4 Cover with a clean damp cloth and put in a warm place to 'sponge' for 40 minutes.
5 Meanwhile, sieve the remaining flour with the salt, cinnamon, nutmeg and sugar.
6 Stir into this the currants and peel, chopped.
7 Melt the butter and beat the egg.
8 Add the dry ingredients to the sponge mixture, pour in the melted butter and beaten egg and mix thoroughly, using the hand.
9 Cover again with a damp cloth and put in a warm place to rise for 1–1$\frac{1}{4}$ hours.
10 Turn the dough on to a floured board and cut into sixteen pieces.
11 Shape each piece into a round bun.
12 Place on a well greased and floured baking sheet, leaving room between each for the buns to spread.
13 Roll the pastry thinly and cut narrow strips about 2 inches long. Place in a cross on top of the buns.
14 Put in a warm place to prove for about 40 minutes.
15 Bake at 425°F.—Mark 7.
16 Five minutes before the end of cooking time, brush each of the buns with a little milk and sugar mixed together.

Crumpets

cooking time   about 10 minutes in all

you will need:

1 lb. flour	pinch of bicarbonate of
½ oz. yeast	soda
1 pint milk or water	1 teaspoon salt

1 Sieve the flour and salt into a bowl and leave in a warm place.
2 Heat liquid until tepid.
3 Cream yeast with a little of the warm liquid. Add the remaining liquid.
4 Pour quickly into the flour and beat well by hand for 5 minutes.
5 Cover and leave in a warm place for an hour.
6 Dissolve bicarbonate in a little warm water. Add to the dough. Beat the dough thoroughly again and put to rise for a further ¾ hour.
7 Grease some crumpet rings or large round cutters and let them heat up on a girdle or electric hot plate.
8 Pour in enough batter to cover the bottom of each ring to a depth of ¼ inch.
9 Cook gently until the top is set. Remove the rings, turn the crumpets over and allow to dry out on the underside for a few minutes.
10 Serve hot with butter, after toasting on both sides.

Chelsea buns

cooking time   20 minutes

you will need:

4 oz. butter	2 eggs
½ pint milk	1 lb. flour
4 oz. sugar	3 oz. currants
1 oz. yeast	1 level teaspoon cinnamon
	or mixed spice

1 Grease a straight-sided tin approximately 10 by 8 inches.
2 Heat the milk with 3 oz. butter, until the butter is just melted.
3 Cream the yeast with 3 oz. sugar, add to the milk.
4 Sieve the flour into a large bowl, make a well in the centre.
5 Beat in the eggs and yeast mixture. Mix by hand to a soft dough.
6 Cover with a damp cloth or a greased polythene bag and leave in a warm place until the dough has doubled its size—1–1½ hours.
7 Turn on to a floured surface and knead well. Roll into an oblong, about 16 × 12 inches.
8 Melt remaining butter, brush over dough, sprinkle with spice, currants and remaining sugar.
9 Roll dough up tightly, as for a Swiss roll, cut into sixteen slices.
10 Place in the prepared tin and leave for 20–30 minutes in a warm place. Bake at 450°F.—Mark 8.
11 Remove from the oven, brush with glaze, cook for another minute.
12 Turn out on a wire tray and leave until cold.
13 Dredge with castor sugar and break the buns apart.

Glaze

Blend 1 tablespoon milk with 1 dessertspoon castor sugar.

Sandwich Cakes

Sandwich cakes seem to be the top favourite cake in this country. They are easy to make, using the creaming method, and there is plenty of scope for varying the mixture. Once you've got the basic recipe right, you can produce a different cake every time by using a new filling or icing.

Victoria sandwich

cooking time   25 minutes

you will need:

4 oz. butter or margarine	4 oz. self-raising flour
4 oz. sugar	water or milk—about
2 eggs	1 tablespoon (optional)*

1 Grease two 7-inch sandwich tins and dust with flour, or line with a round of paper.
2 Cream the fat and sugar.
3 Beat in the egg gradually.
4 Fold in the sieved flour.
5 Divide between the two tins, making sure the mixture is level.
6 Bake on the top shelf of a moderately hot oven 375°F.—Mark 5.
7 Turn out on to a wire rack to cool. When cold, sandwich together with jam, and dust the top with sugar.

*If large eggs are used, additional liquid is not necessary, but water or milk may be added with the egg to give a soft dropping consistency.

For 8-inch sandwich tins you will need: 3 eggs and 6 oz. fat, sugar and self-raising flour. Bake for 30–35 minutes.

Chocolate Victoria sandwich

Make as standard recipe, but sieve 1 oz. cocoa with 3 oz. flour. Fill with butter cream (see page 33) instead of jam.

Orange sandwich cake

Make as standard recipe, adding 1 teaspoon finely grated orange rind to the creamed fat and sugar. Sandwich together with orange butter cream (see page 33) and coat top with orange glacé icing (see page 35).

Clementine cake

Make cake as above, but sandwich with lemon butter cream (see page 33). Top with lemon glacé icing (see page 35) and decorate with crystallised orange and lemon slices.

Apricot almond cake

Make as standard recipe, adding 2–3 drops almond essence to creamed fat and sugar. Sandwich layers with apricot jam and almond butter cream (see page 33).

Small fancy cakes

Using the standard Victoria sandwich recipe, make double the quantity given. Bake mixture in an oblong tin (approximately $10 \times 12 \times 2$ inches). Bake in a moderate oven 350°F.—Mark 4, for 35–40 minutes. Remove cake carefully on to a wire tray. When cold, cut into fancy shapes with a cutter. Cover with glacé icing (see page 34), allowing it to run over the sides of the cakes. Decorate each with halved glacé cherries, walnuts, angelica, silver balls, etc.

Butter sandwich cake

cooking time   30 minutes

you will need:

6 oz. flour	3 eggs
1 teaspoon baking powder	butter icing or jam
6 oz. butter	icing sugar
6 oz. sugar	

1 Grease two 8-inch sandwich tins and dust lightly with flour.
2 Sieve flour and baking powder.
3 Cream butter and sugar until light and fluffy.
4 Gradually beat in the eggs.
5 Lightly fold in the flour.

6 Divide the mixture between the tins. Bake at 375°F.—Mark 5.
7 Turn on to a wire tray and leave to cool.
8 When cold, sandwich with butter cream (see page 33) or jam, and dust top with icing sugar.

Lemon layer cake

Make as before, adding the finely grated rind of 2 lemons to the creamed fat mixture. Divide the mixture between three 7-inch sandwich tins. Bake the cakes for 20 minutes. When cold, sandwich with lemon butter cream (see page 33). Coat the cake with pale coloured lemon glacé icing (see page 35). Decorate with mimosa balls and angelica leaves.

Orange layer cake

Make as for lemon layer cake, using orange rind and juice for flavouring. Tint glacé icing (see page 34) to a pale orange colour with a few drops of red and yellow colouring.

Chocolate frosted layer cake

Make as for lemon or orange layer cake, coating cake with chocolate frosting (see page 36) in place of glacé icing.

Sandwich cake (using oil)

cooking time   35–40 minutes

you will need:

5 oz. flour	7 tablespoons blended
2½ level teaspoons baking	vegetable oil
powder	2 eggs
pinch salt	2½ tablespoons milk
4½ oz. castor sugar	vanilla essence

1 Grease two 7-inch sandwich tins and line with greaseproof paper.
2 Sieve the flour, baking powder, salt and sugar into a bowl.
3 Stir in the oil, the unbeaten eggs, milk and vanilla.
4 Using a wooden spoon, stir until the mixture is smooth and creamy, about 2 minutes.
5 Divide the mixture evenly between the two tins and bake at 350°F.—Mark 4.
6 Cool on a wire tray.
7 When cold, sandwich with jam or lemon curd and sprinkle the top with sieved icing sugar.

Variations of Victoria Sandwich Mixture

1 Make the Victoria sandwich mixture, adding 2 heaped tablespoons ground ginger to the flour before sieving. Place 1 heaped dessertspoon of the mixture in greased patty tins or paper baking cases. Bake in a hot oven 400°F.— Mark 6, for 15–20 minutes. Blend 4 oz. icing sugar with 3 dessertspoons warm water. Beat until smooth. Brush the icing over the buns and return to the oven for 2 minutes until the icing bubbles. Leave on a wire tray to cool.

2 Make the Victoria sandwich mixture. Blend 1 level tablespoons cocoa with 1 tablespoon hot water and stir into the cake mixture. Turn the mixture into an 8-inch cake tin, greased and lined at the bottom with a round of greaseproof paper. Bake 335°F.—Mark 3, on the middle shelf for 35–40 minutes. Turn out on to a wire tray to cool. Coat with orange glacé icing (see page 35). When almost set, sprinkle with coarsely grated chocolate.

Tea-time fancies

Make the Victoria sandwich mixture. Spread the mixture in a Swiss roll tin $7\frac{1}{2} \times 11\frac{1}{2}$ inches, greased and lined. Bake in a moderately hot oven 375°F.—Mark 5, for 20–25 minutes. Turn out on to a wire tray and leave until cold. Trim the edges and cut the cake into 4 strips about 2 inches wide. Cut the remaining cake into 4 or 5 small rounds (use the trimmings of cake to make truffles).

Spread one strip of cake with raspberry jam, sieved. Roll the cake in coconut. Cut into $1\frac{1}{4}$-inch pieces and decorate each with a halved glacé cherry and leaves of angelica.

Coat the second strip of cake with chocolate icing (see page 35) and sprinkle with chopped almonds. Cut into fingers.

Coat the top and sides of the third strip of cake with Vienna icing (see page 35). Cut into $1\frac{1}{4}$-inch fingers and decorate each with a halved walnut. Coat the fourth strip of cake with lemon glacé icing (see page 35) and decorate with segments of crystallised orange.

Brush the tops of the rounds of cake with apricot jam, press a round of almond paste (see page 37) on to each. When set, pipe with butter cream (see page 33).

Truffles

Mix 6 oz. cake crumbs with 2–3 dessertspoons warmed apricot jam and 1 teaspoon almond essence. Divide into 6–8 equal portions. Mould each portion round a glacé or drained Maraschino cherry. Roll in chocolate vermicelli, pressing it on firmly. Leave to set.

Sponge Cakes

Sponge cakes are made by the whisking method. Eggs and sugar are whisked together over hot water until the mixture is a pale lemon colour and slightly thickened. Care should be taken that the bowl containing the mixture does not touch the hot water or the mixture might become overheated. Fat is not usually added to a true sponge, except in the case of a Genoese sponge, when butter which has been clarified is stirred into the eggs and sugar.

Sponge cake

cooking time   10–12 minutes

you will need:

3 oz. flour ($\frac{1}{2}$ level teaspoon baking powder may be added to flour)	4 oz. sugar
	1 tablespoon hot water
3 large eggs	1 oz. butter or margarine (optional)

1 Melt fat, if used. It should be pourable, but not hot.

2 Grease and flour two 7-inch sandwich tins.

3 Sieve flour, and baking powder, if used.

4 Put eggs and sugar in a basin over a pan of hot water, and whisk until thick and creamy.

5 Remove from heat and fold in flour.

6 Stir in water, and fat, if used.

7 Divide between tins, bake near top of a very hot oven, 425°F.—Mark 7.

8 Remove cakes from oven when firm, leave in tins for 1–2 minutes, turn out on a wire tray to cool.

9 When cold, sandwich with jam or a creamy filling (see pages 33–34) and dust with sugar.

Swiss roll

cooking time   7–9 minutes

you will need:

4 oz. flour	1 tablespoon hot water
3 eggs	castor sugar
4 oz. castor sugar	warmed jam

1 Grease a Swiss roll tin (9 × 13 inches) and line with greased greaseproof paper, cut 2 inches larger all round than the tin.
2 Sieve the flour.
3 Whisk the eggs and sugar in a large basin over a pan of hot water. Continue whisking until the mixture is thick and fluffy, and stiff enough to hold the impression of the whisk for a few seconds. Remove from the hot water.
4 Stir in the water and lightly fold in the flour.
5 Put the mixture into the prepared tin, tilting the tin so that the mixture is spread evenly.
6 Bake in a hot oven 425°F.—Mark 7, until golden and springy to touch.
7 Sprinkle a sheet of greaseproof or a damp clean tea-towel with castor sugar. Turn the roll out on to this and remove paper carefully.
8 Using a sharp knife, trim all the crisp outer edges, keeping the shape as neat as possible.
9 Quickly spread the surface of the roll with warmed jam to within ½ inch of the edges.
10 Make a long cut, half way through the depth of the sponge, 1 inch from the near end of the sponge. Roll up the sponge as tightly as possible, using the paper or cloth to keep the roll in shape. Leave the sponge wrapped for a few minutes.
11 Cool on a wire tray and sprinkle with castor sugar.

Chocolate Swiss roll

cooking time   10 minutes

you will need:

2½ oz. flour	1 tablespoon boiling water
½ oz. cocoa	
3 eggs	**filling:**
3 oz. sugar	3 oz. butter
few drops vanilla essence	5 oz. icing sugar

1 Prepare Swiss roll tin as above.
2 Sieve the flour and cocoa.
3 Make as for plain Swiss roll.
4 Bake at 425°F.—Mark 7.
5 Turn out and trim. Place a piece of grease-proof paper on to the sponge and roll up at once. Leave on a wire tray until cold.
6 Beat the butter until soft. Sieve the icing sugar into the bowl containing the butter.

7 Blend the sugar into the butter, adding the essence. Continue to beat until mixture is white and fluffy.
8 Unroll the sponge, spread the filling over the surface and roll up again firmly. Sprinkle the outside of the roll with castor sugar.

Coffee cream roll

Make Swiss roll as before, but roll up without jam and on paper without castor sugar. When the sponge is cold, spread it with coffee butter cream (see page 33) and roll up firmly. Coat the top with glacé icing (see page 34). Decorate with slivers of blanched almonds if liked.

Cherry cream roll

Make Swiss roll as before. Stir chopped glacé cherries into vanilla butter cream (see page 33) and spread over the sponge. Roll up and coat with glacé icing (see page 34). Decorate with halved cherries.

Chocolate rolls

Make Swiss roll mixture as before. Trim and cut in half lengthways. Spread with apricot jam and roll up, starting at the longer sides, making two long thin rolls. Cut each roll into three equal pieces. Place on a wire tray and coat each with chocolate glacé icing (see page 35).

Sponge layer cake

cooking time   1 hour

you will need:

3½ oz. flour	pinch salt
4 eggs	1 oz. melted butter
4 oz. sugar	jam

1 Grease and line a 7-inch cake tin.
2 Sieve flour and salt.
3 Whisk eggs and sugar in a basin over hot water until thick and creamy.
4 Remove bowl from heat and whisk for a further minute until the mixture is stiff enough to hold the mark of the whisk.
5 Fold in half the flour, gently mixing it thoroughly in. Fold in remaining flour.
6 Fold in the melted butter, making sure it is not too hot.
7 Bake at 350°F.—Mark 4. Turn out on to a wire tray to cool.
8 When the cake it cold, cut it through the centre. Spread bottom half with jam, replace top and sprinkle with icing sugar.

Orange layer cake

Make as before, adding the rind of an orange, finely grated, prior to adding the flour. When the cake is cold, cut it through and sandwich with orange butter cream (see page 33). Spread the top with orange glacé icing (see page 35).

Lemon layer cake

Make as before, adding finely grated lemon rind. When cold, cut the cake through, dividing it into three thin layers. Sandwich together with lemon curd and coat with lemon glacé icing (see page 35).

Sponge flan

cooking time   10 minutes

you will need:

3 oz. flour	3 eggs
pinch salt	3 oz. castor sugar

1 Brush an 8-inch sponge flan tin with melted fat or oil. Dust with flour.
2 Sieve flour and salt.
3 Break eggs into a large bowl, add sugar.
4 Place bowl over a pan of hot water and whisk with a wire or rotary beater until mixture is thick and light in colour.
5 Remove from heat and continue whisking until mixture holds the marks made by the whisk— about 1 minute.
6 Fold in half the flour, mixing it in lightly. Add remainder in the same way.
7 Pour into prepared tin and bake in a hot oven 425°F.—Mark 7, until golden and springy to the touch.
8 Turn out on to a wire tray. Fill when cold.

Oriental flan

Bake flan case as above. Drain 1 can mandarin oranges. Arrange the oranges in circles in flan case. Dissolve ½ lemon jelly in a little hot water and make up to ½ pint with juice from the oranges. Leave the jelly until almost setting and then spoon over the fruit and leave to set. Decorate flan with whipped cream and stud with slices of crystallised ginger, if liked.

Fruit salad flan

Bake flan case as above. Fill with assorted fruit, fresh and canned. Fresh fruit should be prepared according to kind (e.g. cherries stoned, grapes seeded, etc.) and canned fruit should be well drained. Cover with glaze and leave to set in a cool place.

Glaze for fruit flans

Use 2 teaspoons arrowroot and ¼ pint sweetened fruit juice or syrup made from ¼ pint water and 2 oz. sugar. Blend arrowroot with a little of the liquid. Bring remaining liquid to boil, stir into blended arrowroot. Return to heat and boil for 1–2 minutes until clear. Add a few drops colouring or lemon juice, if liked. Allow to cool, then spoon carefully over the fruit and leave to set.

Sponge fingers

cooking time   7–10 minutes

you will need:

2 oz. flour	2 oz. castor sugar
2 eggs	castor sugar to dredge

1 Grease and flour a tray of sponge finger tins.
2 Sieve the flour.
3 Whisk the eggs and sugar together in a basin over hot water until thick.
4 Fold in the flour.
5 Turn mixture into the tins, sprinkle well with castor sugar.
6 Bake at 425°F.--Mark 7, until golden and firm.
7 Turn out on to a wire tray to cool.

Lemon sponge fingers

Make as above and when cold sandwich biscuits together in pairs with lemon curd. Dip ends of each in lemon glacé icing (see page 35).

Danish delights

Make sponge fingers as above. Spread thick glacé icing (see page 34) over top of each biscuit and sprinkle thickly with chopped mixed peel.

Chocolate fingers

Make sponge fingers as above. Melt a 2 oz. bar of plain chocolate in a cup. Dip each into the chocolate, allowing the chocolate to come half way up the finger. Stand the biscuits in a small basin or cup, plain side down, until dry.

Sponge drops

Make mixture as for sponge fingers, adding a few drops of vanilla essence to whisked eggs and sugar. Spoon the mixture into a forcing bag, fitted with a plain ½-inch nozzle. Pipe into rounds, well apart, on a greased, floured tin. Bake at 425°F.—Mark 7, for 7–10 minutes, until lightly coloured. Lift carefully on to a wire tray. When cold, dredge with castor sugar.

Genoese sponge

cooking time   about 45 minutes

you will need:

3 oz. butter	3 large eggs
2½ oz. self-raising flour	4 oz. sugar
½ oz. cornflour	

1 Clarify the butter.
2 Grease and line an oblong tin, 10 × 7 × 1 inch deep, or an 8-inch cake tin.
3 Sieve flour and cornflour.
4 Put eggs and sugar into a large bowl and place the bowl over a pan of hot water. Whisk until the mixture is light and thick and will retain the impress of the whisk.
5 Remove bowl from the heat and very lightly fold in half the flour.
6 Fold in the remaining flour alternately with the cooled butter.
7 Bake in a moderately hot oven 375°F.—Mark 5, until golden brown and firm to the touch.
8 Turn on to a wire tray to cool.
  This mixture may be used to make oblong layer cakes or gâteaux. Make as many layers as required, and when cold sandwich together with whipped cream or butter cream (see page 33). Coat with glacé icing (see page 34) or frosting (see page 43) and decorate as liked.
  Alternatively, cut the sponge into fingers or fancy shapes when cold. Ice and decorate as liked.

To clarify butter

Place butter in a pan with cold water. Heat slowly until the butter melts. Strain into a bowl and leave until the butter sets on top of the water. Remove the butter and scrape off the sediment from the underside. Put the clarified butter in a small bowl and leave in a warm place so that it is melted and ready for use. Do not allow the butter to become hot.

Chocolate Genoese

cooking time   45 minutes

you will need:

4 oz. sugar	1 level tablespoon cocoa
3 eggs	3 tablespoons blended
3 oz. flour	vegetable oil

1 Grease and line an 8-inch cake tin.
2 Whisk the eggs and sugar in a bowl over hot water.
3 Fold in the flour, sieved with the cocoa, alternately with the oil.
4 Pour into the prepared tin and bake at 375°F.—Mark 5.

5 Allow to cool in the tin for a few minutes, then turn on to a wire tray.
6 Cut the cake through and sandwich together with a creamy filling (see pages 33 and 34).

Continental cakes

you will need:

Genoese sponge	glacé icing (made with
butter cream (made with	12 oz. icing sugar) (see
4 oz. butter) (see page 33)	page 34)

1 Flavour the butter cream with a few drops vanilla essence and tint with red colouring to a pale pink.
2 Cut the sponge into rounds 1½ inches in diameter.
3 Pile butter icing on top of each round. Smooth with the back of a teaspoon to form a dome shape.
4 Place cakes on a wire tray over a large plate. Leave until the butter cream is firm.
5 Coat with white glacé icing. Allow the icing to run down the sides of the cake so that they are completely covered. The butter cream should just show through.
6 If liked, pipe with butter cream when the icing has set.
7 Serve the cakes in small paper cases.
  Alternatively, cut the Genoese sponge layer through the centre. Sandwich together with butter cream and cut into rounds. Coat with glacé icing and decorate with crystallised violets, rose petals and silver balls.

Parisian cakes

you will need:

Genoese sponge	glacé icing (see page 34)
apricot jam	butter cream (see page 33)
almond paste (see page 37)	silver balls, etc., or
	decoration

1 Cut the Genoese into rounds 1½ inches in diameter.
2 Brush the tops of each with warmed apricot jam.
3 Make domes of almond paste, slightly smaller than the top of the cakes. Press firmly into position.
4 Finish as for continental cakes.

Mayfair cakes

you will need:

Genoese sponge	chocolate vermicelli or
Whipped cream or butter	coarsely grated plain
cream (see page 33)	chocolate
	walnuts (optional)

1 Cut the Genoese into rounds 1½ inches in diameter.
2 Spread top and sides of each with cream or butter cream.
3 Roll in vermicelli or grated chocolate.
4 Press the chocolate into position with a knife.
5 Pipe a large rose of cream on top of each and decorate with a halved walnut, if liked.

Rum cakes

you will need:

Genoese sponge
rum
apricot jam

almond paste (see page 73)
glacé icing (see page 34)
or icing sugar

1 Sprinkle Genoese with rum. Cut into 1½-inch squares.
2 Brush with warm apricot jam.
3 Cover top and sides of each with almond paste, rolled thinly.
4 Spoon a little glacé icing over the top of each or dust with icing sugar.

Genoese almond fingers

you will need:

Genoese sponge
shredded toasted almonds

coffee butter cream (see page 33)
icing sugar

1 Spread the sponge with coffee butter cream. Rough up with the prongs of a fork.
2 Sprinkle with almonds and press lightly into position with a palette knife.
3 Dredge with icing sugar.
4 Cut into fingers, 1 × 3 inches.

Clementine fingers

Make as above, spreading the sponge with lemon butter cream (see page 33). Sprinkle with chopped peel instead of almonds and omit the icing sugar.

Genoese sponge cake

cooking time   about 40 minutes

you will need:

8 oz. self-raising flour
8 oz. butter

4 eggs
8 oz. castor sugar

1 Clarify the butter.
2 Grease and line two 9-inch sandwich tins.
3 Sieve the flour.
4 Put eggs and sugar in a large bowl over a pan of hot water. Whisk until light and thick.
5 Remove from heat. Fold in flour and butter alternately.
6 Pour the mixture quickly into the tins and bake in a moderately hot oven, 375° F.—Mark 5, until golden brown and firm.
7 Turn on to a wire tray to cool.
This makes a firmer cake than the Genoese sponge and is more suitable for gâteaux and layer cakes. Split each layer through and sandwich together with a creamy filling (see pages 33 and 34). Coat with glacé icing (see page 34) or butter cream (see page 33). This cake may also be covered with thin almond paste (see page 37) and decorated.

Chocolate Genoese sponge cake

Make as above, adding 2 oz. melted chocolate to the thick egg and sugar mixture, whisking it in before adding the flour.

Coffee Genoese sponge cake

Make as above, adding 1 tablespoon coffee essence to the whisked egg and sugar mixture.

Quick-Mix Cakes

Modern ingredients make new methods possible, and now you can mix up a cake so quickly that you'll be able to claim truthfully that it didn't take a minute. Try these easy recipes for making tea-time cakes the modern way.

It is important with these quick mix recipes that the ingredients are at room temperature, so don't forget to take them out of the refrigerator at least an hour before you are ready to start.

One-stage cake

cooking time   25–35 minutes

you will need:

4 oz. self-raising flour	4 oz. sugar
1 level teaspoon baking powder	2 eggs
4 oz. soft margarine	filling and icing as liked

1 Grease two 7-inch sandwich tins and line the bottom of each with a round of greaseproof paper.
2 Sieve flour and baking powder into a bowl.
3 Put the margarine and sugar into the bowl.
4 Break the eggs into the bowl. Mix all the ingredients together with a wooden spoon—this should take about 1 minute.
5 Divide the mixture between the tins. Bake at 335°F.—Mark 3, on the middle shelf.
6 When the cakes are cold, sandwich together with filling and coat the top with icing.
If liked, the cake may be baked in one 8-inch cake tin, greased and with the bottom lined with greaseproof paper. Cook for 35–45 minutes.

Suggested icings:
Chocolate icing, see page 35.
Orange icing, see page 35.
Coffee icing, see page 35.

Festival layer cake

cooking time   35–45 minutes

you will need:

8 oz. self-raising flour	4 oz. ground almonds
8 oz. soft margarine	4 oz. sugar
8 oz. sugar	red and green colouring
4 eggs	glacé icing (see page 34)

filling:
4 oz. butter

1 Grease two 8-inch sandwich tins and line the bottom of each with a round of greaseproof paper.
2 Make the cake as for one-stage cake. Bake on the middle shelf at 335°F.—Mark 3.
3 Turn the cakes on to a wire tray to become cold.
4 To make the filling, cream the butter and sugar and beat in the almonds.
5 Colour $\frac{1}{3}$ of the filling pink and the remainder green with a few drops of colouring.
6 Cut through each cake, sandwich together again with green filling.
7 Sandwich these together with the pink filling.
8 Coat the cake with glacé icing, tinted pink with a few drops of red colouring. Decorate as liked.

One-stage chocolate cake

cooking time   20–25 minutes

you will need:

4 oz. luxury margarine	**filling:**
5 oz. sugar	2 oz. plain chocolate
4 oz. self-raising flour	2 oz. soft margarine
1 heaped tablespoon cocoa	1 oz. castor sugar
2 eggs	2 dessertspoons hot water
1 tablespoon milk	1 dessertspoon milk

1 Grease two 7-inch sandwich tins, grease and line the bottom of each.
2 Put margarine and sugar into a mixing bowl.
3 Sieve flour and cocoa on to fat and sugar.
4 Mix in the eggs and milk.
5 Beat all together with a wooden spoon for 2 minutes.
6 Divide the mixture between the tins and smooth the tops.
7 Bake in the middle of a moderate oven 350°F.—Mark 4.
8 Turn on to a wire tray to cool.
9 Melt chocolate in a small bowl over hot water. Allow to cool.
10 Add margarine and sugar and whisk for 1–2 minutes.
11 Add the water, then milk, then whisk again.
12 Sandwich the cakes together with filling and dust the top with sugar.

One-stage fruit cake

cooking time   2–2$\frac{1}{4}$ hours

you will need:

12 oz. self-raising flour	12 oz. mixed dried fruit
6 oz. soft margarine	3 eggs
6 oz. sugar	4 tablespoons milk
1$\frac{1}{2}$ level teaspoons mixed spice	

1 Grease and line a round 7-inch cake tin.
2 Place all the ingredients in a large mixing bowl.
3 Beat together for about 1 minute until all the ingredients are well mixed.
4 Place the mixture in the prepared tin.
5 Smooth the top of the mixture.
6 Bake in the middle of a very moderate oven 335°F.—Mark 3.
7 Remove and cool on a wire tray.

One-stage cherry cakes

cooking time   15–20 minutes

you will need:

4 oz. self-raising flour	1 level teaspoon baking powder
4 oz. soft margarine	$\frac{1}{4}$ pint double cream
4 oz. sugar	fresh cherries
2 eggs	

1 Place 12–16 paper cases on a baking tray.

2 Sieve the flour and baking powder into a mixing bowl. Add the other ingredients.

3 Quickly mix together, then beat thoroughly with a wooden spoon (pressing the margarine to the sides of the bowl if it has been in the refrigerator).

4 Put the mixture into the paper cases and bake near the top of a moderately hot oven 375°F.— Mark 5.

5 Cool on a wire tray.

6 When cakes are cold, pipe or swirl a spoonful of whipped cream on to each and decorate with fresh cherries.

Minute-mix cakes

These 'minute-mix' cakes are also made in one stage. No creaming is required. Their success depends on the use of a quick creaming fat, so choose soft margarine.

Method of making minute-mix cakes

1 Grease two 8-inch sandwich tins and line the bottom of each with a round of greaseproof paper.

2 Chop up the margarine in a mixing bowl.

3 Sieve in the dry ingredients.

4 Add the sugar, eggs, essence or flavouring and the milk.

5 Beat well for 1 minute, until evenly mixed, adding another spoonful of milk if necessary to make a dropping consistency.

6 Spread the mixture into the two tins.

7 Bake until firm, then turn on to a wire tray to cool.

8 When cold, sandwich with butter cream (see page 33) and ice and decorate as liked.

Orange layer cake

you will need:

8 oz. self-raising flour	6 oz. margarine
pinch salt	3 eggs
1 level teaspoon baking powder	rind 1 orange, finely grated
6 oz. castor sugar	about 3 tablespoons milk

Method as in previous column.

Lemon layer cake

you will need:

The same ingredients as for orange layer cake, using lemon rind instead of orange rind. Method as in previous column.

Chocolate cake

you will need:

6 oz. self-raising flour	6 oz. castor sugar
pinch salt	6 oz. margarine
4 level tablespoons cocoa	3 eggs
small pinch bicarbonate of soda	$\frac{1}{4}$ teaspoon vanilla essence
	about 3 tablespoons milk

Method as in previous column.

Coconut cake

you will need:

6 oz. self-raising flour	6 oz. margarine
pinch salt	3 eggs
1 level teaspoon baking powder	$\frac{1}{4}$ teaspoon vanilla essence
6 oz. castor sugar	2 oz. desiccated coconut
	about 4 tablespoons milk

The cooking time for each of these cakes is 20 minutes. Bake in a moderately hot oven 375°F.—Mark 5, on the third shelf from the top.

Layer Cakes and Gâteaux

These are usually made from Victoria sandwich or sponge cake mixtures, and are filled with cream or butter cream and coated with icing or frosting. These cakes should be made on the day that they are to be eaten, but if this is not possible and the cake must be made the day before, it should be wrapped in foil or greaseproof when cold, and then filled and iced when required.

Chocolate layer cake

cooking time   20 minutes

you will need:

8 oz. flour	3 oz. plain chocolate
2 level teaspoons baking powder	1 tablespoon milk
6 oz. margarine	4 eggs
6 oz. castor sugar	pinch salt

1 Grease three 7-inch sandwich tins and dust with flour.
2 Sieve flour, baking powder and salt.
3 Melt chocolate in milk in a basin over a small pan hot water. Allow to cool.
4 Cream margarine and sugar.
5 Beat in melted chocolate and eggs.
6 Fold in sieved flour.
7 Divide the mixture between the prepared tins.
8 Bake at 375°F.—Mark 5. Turn cakes out on to a wire tray and leave until cold.
9 Sandwich cakes together with walnut or almond butter cream (see page 33).
10 Coat top with vanilla glacé icing (see page 34) and decorate with walnuts or almonds, depending on which butter cream is used.

Seville layer cake

Make chocolate layer cake as above, adding 1 teaspoon finely grated orange rind to the creamed fat and sugar. Sandwich cakes together with orange butter cream (see page 33).
Coat top with orange glacé icing (see page 35) and decorate with coarsely grated plain chocolate.

Ginger layer cake

cooking time   15–20 minutes

you will need:

4 oz. self-raising flour	2 eggs
1 rounded teaspoon ground ginger	
½ level teaspoon baking powder	**filling:**
4 oz. luxury margarine	3 oz. soft margarine
4 oz. castor sugar	8 oz. icing sugar, sieved
	3 dessertspoons milk
	2 oz. crystallised ginger

1 Brush a Swiss roll tin 11 × 8 inches with melted margarine and line with greaseproof paper.
2 Sieve the flour, ginger and baking powder into a mixing bowl.
3 Add the margarine and castor sugar and the eggs, and beat well for 1 minute with a wooden spoon.
4 Place the mixture in the tin and smooth the top.
5 Bake in a moderately hot oven 375°F.—Mark 5, on the second shelf from the top.

6 Cool on a wire tray.
7 Make the filling. Place the margarine, icing sugar and milk in a mixing bowl. Beat together thoroughly.
8 Chop the ginger very finely, reserving five whole pieces for decoration.
9 Add the chopped ginger to the filling and beat together.
10 Cut the cake into three even-sized pieces (cutting across the cake).
11 Trim the outside edges and sandwich together with the ginger filling, saving enough to go on the top.
12 Spread the top of the cake with the filling and mark with a knife to give a swirled effect. Place the whole pieces of ginger down the centre of the cake.
If liked, the filling can be made with stem ginger. Use 3 dessertspoons of the syrup instead of the milk and top the cake with slices of stem ginger.

Neapolitan layer cake

cooking time   35–45 minutes

you will need:

8 oz. luxury margarine	6 oz. soft margarine
8 oz. castor sugar	2 tablespoons milk
4 eggs	2 oz. glacé cherries
8 oz. self-raising flour	1 oz. walnuts
	2 pineapple rings, well drained
filling:	
1 lb. icing sugar, sieved	stick angelica

1 Place all the cake ingredients together in a mixing bowl.
2 Beat for 1 minute with a wooden spoon.
3 Place the mixture in two 8-inch sandwich tins, greased and the bottom lined with a round of greaseproof paper. Smooth the top of the mixture.
4 Bake in the middle of a very moderate oven 335°F.—Mark 3. Cool on a wire tray.
5 Make the filling. Place the icing sugar, margarine and milk in a mixing bowl. Beat thoroughly together.
6 Chop the cherries (reserving two for decoration), walnuts, pineapple and angelica. Mix together and add to the filling. Beat together thoroughly.
7 Cut through the centre of each cake.
8 Sandwich together with the filling (keeping enough for the top), making three layers of filling.
9 Spread the remaining filling on the top of the cake.
10 Decorate with the remaining chopped cherries.

Coconut layer cake

cooking time   25–30 minutes

you will need:

4 oz. self-raising flour	4 oz. desiccated coconut
4 oz. margarine	milk to mix
4 oz. castor sugar	8 oz. apricot jam
2 eggs	glacé icing (see page 34)

1 Grease two 7-inch sandwich tins and line the bottom of the tins with greaseproof paper.
2 Sieve the flour.
3 Cream the fat and sugar.
4 Beat in the eggs.
5 Fold in the flour and 2 oz. of the coconut, using a little milk to give a soft dropping mixture.
6 Turn into tins and bake in the centre of the oven 375°F.—Mark 5. Allow to cool on a wire tray.
7 Sandwich the cakes with some of the jam and spread the rest round the edges of the cake.
8 Place the rest of the coconut on a piece of greaseproof paper. Roll the sides of the cake in the coconut.
9 Spread thick glacé icing over the top of the cake.

Chocolate gâteau

cooking time   45 minutes

you will need:

3 oz. plain flour	chocolate butter cream (see page 33)
1 level tablespoon cocoa	white glacé icing (see page 34)
3 eggs	
4 oz. castor sugar	
3 tablespoons blended vegetable oil	grated plain chocolate or chocolate drops for decorating

1 Grease and line an 8-inch deep cake tin.
2 Sieve flour and cocoa.
3 Break the eggs into a bowl and whisk well.
4 Stir in castor sugar and place bowl over a pan of hot water. Whisk until thick and frothy. Remove from heat.
5 Fold in the sieved flour alternately with the oil, mixing thoroughly.
6 Pour into the prepared tin. Bake at 375°F.—Mark 5.
7 Allow cake to cool in the tin for 5 minutes before turning out on to a wire tray.
8 When cake is cold, cut through the centre, using a saw-edged knife, if available.
9 Sandwich together with chocolate butter cream.
10 Coat with white glacé icing, flavoured with vanilla. When almost set, decorate with grated chocolate or chocolate drops.

Party-time cake

cooking time   12–15 minutes

you will need:

3 eggs	**filling:**
1½ tablespoons milk	3 oz. butter
½ teaspoon vanilla essence	3 tablespoons lemon curd
6 oz. castor sugar	6 oz. icing sugar, sieved
6 oz. self-raising flour	1 dessertspoon hot water
1½ teaspoons baking powder	glacé icing (see page 34)
3 oz. butter, melted	

1 Whisk the eggs, milk and essence together in a bowl.
2 Gradually add the sugar.
3 Fold in the flour, sieved with the baking powder.
4 Stir in the melted butter lightly, making sure it is well blended in.
5 Divide the mixture between two well-greased 7-inch sandwich tins.
6 Bake at 375°F.—Mark 5. Cool in the tins for 5 minutes before turning out.
7 Make the filling. Cream the butter and sugar, then add the lemon curd and hot water. Beat until smooth.
8 Sandwich the cakes together when cold with the filling and coat the cake with glacé icing.

Coffee cream cake

cooking time   30–35 minutes

you will need:

8 oz. self-raising flour	**filling:** (see overleaf)
pinch salt	6 oz. butter
8 oz. butter	12 oz. icing sugar
8 oz. sugar	4 heaped teaspoons instant coffee
rind and juice 1 small lemon	1 dessertspoon boiling water
4 eggs	2 oz. chopped walnuts
1 tablespoon water	

1 Grease and line two 8-inch sandwich tins and line the bottom of each with a round of greaseproof paper.
2 Sieve flour and salt.
3 Cream the fat and sugar, add the lemon rind, finely grated.
4 Separate the egg yolks from the whites. Beat yolks into the creamed mixture a little at a time.
5 Fold in the flour, adding the lemon juice and water to make a soft dropping consistency.
6 Whisk egg whites until stiff, fold into the mixture.
7 Divide the mixture between the two tins, smooth the tops with a palette knife.
8 Bake in a moderately hot oven 375°F.—Mark 5 until golden.
9 Turn out on to a wire tray and leave until cold.

10 Sandwich together with half the filling, spread remainder on top of the cake.

To make the filling:

1 Cream the butter until soft.

2 Add the sieved icing sugar, beat until smooth.

3 Dissolve the coffee in the boiling water and beat into the creamed butter and sugar.

4 Add the chopped walnuts and mix thoroughly.

Mocha gâteau

Make cake as before, sandwich together with coffee butter cream (see page 33). Coat with coffee glacé icing (see page 35) and decorate with halved walnuts.

Coffee and chestnut gâteau

cooking time   40–45 minutes

you will need:

4 oz. self-raising flour	2 oz. coffee butter cream
4 oz. butter or margarine	(see page 33)
4 oz. sugar	coffee glacé icing (see
2 large eggs	page 35)
4 oz. cooked chestnuts, sieved	marrons glacés (optional)

1 Grease and line a 6-inch square tin.

2 Sieve the flour.

3 Cream the fat and sugar, gradually beat in the eggs.

4 Fold in the flour and 2 oz. of the chestnuts.

5 Turn into the prepared tin and bake at 335°F.—Mark 3 until firm and golden. Cool on a wire tray.

6 Cream the remaining chestnuts with the butter cream.

7 Cut the cake through the centre and sandwich together with about half the butter cream mixture.

8 Spread thick coffee glacé icing over the top of the cake. When set, pipe with remaining butter cream and decorate with marrons glacés, if liked.

Tyrolean coffee gâteau

cooking time   40 minutes

you will need:

6 oz. flour	2 tablespoons coffee
½ level teaspoon salt	essence
2 level teaspoons baking powder	a little milk
	glazing syrup (see below)
5 oz. soft brown sugar	chopped nuts
2 eggs	¼ pint double cream
7 tablespoons corn oil	

1 Grease a tin approximately $8\frac{1}{2} \times 1\frac{1}{2}$ inches and line the bottom with a piece of greased greaseproof paper.

2 Sieve the dry ingredients into a bowl.

3 Whisk together the egg yolks, corn oil and coffee essence, made up to 7 tablespoons with milk. Add to the dry ingredients.

4 Beat well to form a smooth, slack batter, then fold in the stiffly beaten egg whites.

5 Turn the mixture into the prepared tin and bake in a moderately hot oven, 375°F.—Mark 5. Turn out and leave until cold.

6 When the cake is cold, return it to the cake tin. Pour the hot glazing syrup over and leave overnight.

7 Turn the cake out on to a serving dish and spread with the cream, whisked until thick and flavoured with coffee essence. Decorate with chopped nuts.

Glazing syrup

Boil 4 oz. sugar and ¼ pint strong black coffee briskly for 5 minutes. Remove from the heat and stir in 2 tablespoons brandy.

Tyrolean chocolate gâteau

cooking time   40 minutes

you will need:

5 oz. flour	2 eggs
1 oz. cocoa	3½ fluid oz. corn oil
½ level teaspoon salt	3½ fluid oz. milk
2 level teaspoons baking powder	½ teaspoon vanilla essence
	¼ pint double cream
5 oz. soft brown sugar	glazing syrup (see below)

1 Grease a tin approximately $8\frac{1}{2} \times 11\frac{1}{2}$ inches and line the bottom with a piece of greased greaseproof paper.

2 Sieve the dry ingredients into a bowl.

3 Whisk the egg yolks, corn oil, milk and essence together and add to the dry ingredients. Beat well to form a smooth, slack batter.

4 Fold in the stiffly beaten egg whites.

5 Turn the mixture into the prepared tin and bake in a moderately hot oven 375°F.—Mark 5. Turn out and leave until cold.

6 When the cake is cold, return it to the tin and pour over the hot glazing syrup. Leave overnight.

7 Turn the cake out on to a serving dish. Cover with the cream, whisked until thick, and sprinkle the cake with grated chocolate.

Glazing syrup

Boil 4 oz. sugar with ¼ pint water briskly for 5 minutes. Remove from the heat and stir in 2 tablespoons rum.

Macaroon ring gâteau

cooking time   35 minutes

you will need:

2–3 large macaroon biscuits	**filling:**
	½ pint double cream
4 oz. self-raising flour	sugar (optional)
4 eggs	vanilla essence (optional)
4 oz. sugar	small can fruit salad
½ teaspoon almond essence	

1 Bake macaroons in a moderate oven until darker in colour and brittle. Crush with a rolling pin.
2 Brush a 9-inch ring tin well with butter and sprinkle evenly with macaroon crumbs.
3 Sieve the flour.
4 Separate the eggs. Whisk the whites until stiff, then gradually whisk in yolks and sugar. Add the almond essence.
5 Place the bowl of egg mixture over boiling water and continue whisking until the mixture is thick and creamy.
6 Remove from the heat and continue whisking until the mixture is cool to the touch.
7 Fold in the flour, stirring gently until it is well mixed.
8 Pour into the prepared tin. Bake in a moderate oven 350°F.—Mark 4, on the second shelf down until firm to the touch.
9 Turn out and cool on a wire tray. When cold, cut through with a sharp knife, making two layers.
10 Place bottom layer on a serving plate. Whip the cream until thick. Stir in sugar and vanilla essence to taste, if liked. Fold in drained fruit salad. Spread filling over bottom layer, top with second layer and leave in a cold place until required.

Tipsy macaroon gâteau

Make as above, omitting fruit. Soak bottom layer with sherry or rum before spreading with cream.

Gâteau surprise

cooking time   10–15 minutes

you will need:

3½ oz. flour	2 oz. glacé cherries
½ oz. cocoa	6 oz. butter or margarine
4 eggs	6 oz. icing sugar
4 oz. castor sugar	lemon flavoured white
2 oz. chocolate	glacé icing (see page 35)
2 oz. blanched almonds	

1 Grease and flour an oblong tin measuring 5 × 7 inches.
2 Sieve the flour and cocoa.
3 Whisk the eggs and sugar over hot water until thick and creamy.
4 Fold flour into the whisked mixture, pour into the tin and bake in a very hot oven 450°F.—Mark 8.
5 Place on a wire tray until cold.
6 Cut an oblong piece from the top of the cake, using a sharp knife. Cut an inch in from the edge and a good ½ inch deep. Remove this 'slice' carefully. Scoop out centre of cake with a teaspoon to make a 'box'. Place cake on a serving plate.
7 Roughly chop the chocolate, almonds and cherries, saving a few almonds and cherries for decoration.
8 Cream together the butter and icing sugar and beat in the chocolate, chopped almonds and cherries.
9 Spread this mixture into the hollow of the cake. Carefully replace slice or lid, and press down into position.
10 Coat top of cake with lemon flavoured white glacé icing. Decorate with remaining cherries and almonds.
11 Leave in a cool place for several hours before slicing.

Orange and chocolate gâteau

cooking time   25–30 minutes

you will need:

4 oz. self-raising flour	finely grated rind 1 orange
4 oz. luxury margarine	chocolate cream
4 oz. castor sugar	1 can mandarin oranges
2 eggs	chocolate vermicelli

1 Grease and line the bottom of two 7-inch sandwich tins.
2 Sieve the flour.
3 Cream the margarine and sugar until light and fluffy.
4 Add the eggs one at a time, beating well after each addition.
5 Beat in the orange rind.
6 Gently fold in the flour with a metal spoon.
7 Turn the mixture into the two prepared tins and bake in a moderately hot oven 375°F.—Mark 5.
8 Remove from the oven and turn out on to a wire tray to cool.
9 Spread one of the cakes with half the chocolate cream and cover with half the mandarin oranges, well drained.
10 Top with the other cake.
11 Spread the top and sides with chocolate cream. Press chocolate vermicelli round the sides.
12 Using the remaining chocolate cream, pipe rosettes round the edge of the top of the cake and decorate with remaining mandarin oranges.

Chocolate cream

you will need:

4 oz. soft margarine	few drops vanilla essence
6 oz. icing sugar	1 dessertspoon milk
2 level dessertspoons cocoa	

1 Sieve the sugar and cocoa together into a bowl.
2 Add the margarine and cream until light and smooth.
3 Add the milk and essence and beat in thoroughly.

Raspberry gâteau

you will need:

2 8-inch rounds of sponge or sandwich cake	½ pint double cream thick white glacé icing,
8 oz. raspberries	lemon flavoured (see
2 oz. castor sugar	page 35)

1 Mash half the raspberries with the castor sugar.
2 Spread over one cake, top with cream, whisked until thick, and cover with second round of cake.
3 Coat with thick glacé icing and decorate with remaining raspberries.
4 Serve as soon as the icing is set.

Mandarin gâteau

Make as above, using drained mandarin oranges in place of raspberries and omitting the castor sugar. Sprinkle the icing with coarsely grated chocolate and decorate with mandarins.

Strawberry meringue gâteau

Make as above, using strawberries instead of raspberries, piling more whipped cream with the strawberries on top of the cake. Decorate with small whole meringues or pieces of meringue.

Caramel coffee gâteau

you will need:

2 rounds sponge or sandwich cake	6 oz. sugar ¼ pint water
coffee butter cream (see page 33)	split blanched almonds

1 Split sandwich cakes and sandwich the four layers together with coffee butter cream.
2 Dissolve the sugar in the water, bring to the boil, then simmer gently until golden brown. Allow bubbles to die down.
3 Place cake on a wire tray, pour half the caramel on to the top and allow it to cover the surface. Swirl with a knife while soft. Decorate with almonds.

4 Pour the remaining caramel into a shallow greased tin. Allow to set, then crush and mix with chopped almonds.
5 When the top of the cake is set, lightly spread coffee butter cream round the sides and roll in crushed almonds and caramel.

Chocolate curl cake

you will need:

1 Genoese or Victoria sandwich (square or oblong) cake	chocolate curls lemon flavoured white glacé icing (see page 35)
chocolate butter cream (see page 33)	

1 Cut the cake through and sandwich with chocolate butter cream.
2 Spread butter cream on sides, if liked, and rough up with a fork.
3 Coat top with thick glacé icing.
4 When set, sprinkle with chocolate curls.

Chocolate curls

Melt 4 oz. chocolate in a basin over a pan of hot water. Spread in a thin layer over a cold surface. Allow to become firm, but not set completely. Hold a long-bladed knife vertically and pull it over the chocolate so that the knife gently 'scrapes up' the chocolate, which will flake and roll into long curls. Place curls on a plate until required. Handle them with care as they are very fragile.

Almond mocha cake

Cut a chocolate cake in half and fill with coffee butter cream (see page 33). Stand the cake on a wire tray and coat all over with chocolate glacé icing (see page 35). When the icing is firm, pipe coffee butter cream, using a large star nozzle, in lines across the top of the cake and round the top edge. Stud the butter cream with halved toasted almonds.

Chocolate swirl cake

Sandwich two rounds of chocolate sponge cake with orange or lemon butter cream (see page 33). Place on a wire tray and coat outside with white American frosting (see page 35). Swirl roughly with a spatula. Spoon drops of melted chocolate at intervals all round the top. Swirl with a small knife or the back of a spoon, so that the chocolate streaks the white frosting.

Make two 7 or 8-inch cakes, using Victoria, Genoese or one-stage cake recipes. Cut each cake through and sandwich together with one of the following fillings. Spread the top of the cake, or coat the whole cake, with glacé icing (see page 34).

1 Cream 6 oz. butter with 6 oz. castor sugar. Beat in 6 oz. ground almonds. Add lemon juice or essence to taste.
2 Melt 4 oz. grated chocolate. Stir in 3 tablespoons blended vegetable oil and 3 tablespoons milk. Beat this mixture into 10 oz. sieved icing sugar.
3 Sieve 6 oz. icing sugar with 2 dessertspoons cocoa. Cream 4 oz. luxury margarine with the sugar and cocoa. Beat in 1 dessertspoon milk and add vanilla essence to taste.
4 Sieve 14 oz. icing sugar. Cream 3 oz. cream cheese. Gradually work the icing sugar into the cheese. Add 1–2 dessertspoons lemon juice.
5 Cream 4 oz. butter with 6 oz. sieved icing sugar. Add 2 chopped, drained, canned pineapple rings and 2 oz. chopped glacé cherries.
6 Melt 4 oz. plain chocolate with 2 oz. butter in a pan over hot water. Remove from the heat and gradually stir in 12 oz. sieved icing sugar, 4 tablespoons boiling water and peppermint essence to taste.

Icings, Fillings and Frostings

Eyes light up with pleasure when there is a gorgeous cake on the table. Who but you will know that it's an ordinary Victoria sandwich or sponge cake that you've transformed with one of these fillings and icings?

Butter cream

you will need:

6–8 oz. icing sugar   vanilla essence
4 oz. butter

1 Sieve the icing sugar.
2 Beat butter with a wooden spoon or spatula until soft.
3 Beat icing sugar into the butter, adding a few drops of vanilla essence. The amount of icing sugar needed will depend on the consistency of the cream required.

Orange or lemon butter cream

Add finely grated lemon or orange rind and juice to taste to the creamed butter and sugar. Beat hard to prevent curdling.

Mock cream

you will need:

4 oz. butter   3 tablespoons boiling water
4 oz. castor sugar   2 tablespoons cold milk

1 Cream the butter and sugar until light in colour and shiny.
2 Beat in the boiling water, a drop at a time.
3 Gradually add the milk in the same way.
4 Leave in a cold place until firm.

Coffee butter cream

Make as basic butter cream. Omit the vanilla essence and use 2 teaspoons coffee essence.

Coffee essence

Blend 3 tablespoons instant coffee with 2 tablespoons lemon juice or rum. Dissolve 8 oz. sugar in $\frac{3}{4}$ pint water and bring to the boil. Boil for 10 minutes. Pour the boiling syrup on to the coffee mixture, stirring. When cold, pour into a screw-top bottle and store in a cool place. Use as required.

Almond butter cream

Add 2 tablespoons finely chopped toasted almonds to creamed butter and sugar.

Chocolate butter cream

Melt a 2 oz. bar plain chocolate. Beat 2 oz. butter until soft. Blend in the melted chocolate and 3 oz. sieved icing sugar.

Mocha butter cream

Make as coffee butter cream, adding 2 oz. melted chocolate as well as the coffee essence.

Walnut butter cream

Add 2 tablespoons finely chopped walnuts to creamed butter and sugar, and mix in thoroughly.

Continental cream

you will need:

½ pint cream	1½ oz. icing sugar
1–2 egg yolks	½ teaspoon vanilla essence

1 Sieve the icing sugar.
2 Whisk the cream until thick.
3 Beat the egg yolks with the sugar, adding the vanilla essence.
4 Fold the yolk mixture into the cream, mixing thoroughly.

French cream filling

you will need:

2 oz. castor sugar	½ pint and 1 tablespoon milk
1 oz. flour	
2 egg yolks	2 or 3 drops almond essence

1 Mix sugar and flour together. Blend with the egg yolks, the tablespoon milk and the essence.
2 Bring the half pint of milk to the boil, pour on to the blended mixture, stirring well.
3 Rinse the pan with cold water, pour the mixture back into the pan.
4 Heat gently until the mixture boils, stirring throughout.
5 Boil for 3 minutes, remove from the heat and leave until cold.

Apricot cream filling

you will need:

8 oz. dried apricots	4 oz. icing sugar
2 oz. butter	

1 Soak apricots overnight. Stew in a little water, drain, sieve and allow to cool.
2 Sieve the sugar.
3 Cream the butter and beat in the sugar.
4 Beat in the apricot purée, adding a little more sugar if the mixture is too soft.

Chocolate filling

Blend 2 oz. butter with 2 oz. melted chocolate, cooled. Beat in 2 oz. ground almonds and 2 oz. sugar.

Chocolate rum filling

Make as above, adding rum or rum essence to taste.

Coconut filling

Blend 2 oz. sieved icing sugar with 1 egg yolk, and 1 tablespoon lemon juice. Heat gently in a basin over a pan of hot water until thick—about 5 minutes. Remove from the heat, stir in 1 oz. desiccated coconut. Allow to cool before using.

Rum and walnut filling

Cream 2 oz. butter with 3 oz. brown sugar. Gradually beat in 2 dessertspoons rum to taste. Stir in 2 oz. chopped walnuts.

Cream filling

Blend ½ oz. cornflour with a little milk, taken from ¼ pint. Bring the rest to the boil, pour on to the blended cornflour stirring. Return the mixture to the pan. Cook for 3 minutes, stirring throughout. Leave to cool. Cream 1 oz. butter with 1 oz. sugar. Gradually beat in the cornflour mixture. Beat well, add 2–3 drops vanilla essence. Allow to become cold before using.

Apricot nut filling

you will need:

4 tablespoons sieved apricot jam	1 tablespoon chopped walnuts
4 tablespoons ground almonds	1 teaspoon vanilla essence (optional)

Mix all the ingredients together thoroughly.

Date and lemon filling

you will need:

2 oz. sugar	2 oz. chopped nuts
2 tablespoons water	lemon juice or essence
2 oz. cake crumbs	

1 Heat the sugar in the water until dissolved.
2 Stir in the crumbs and dates.
3 Add lemon juice or lemon essence to taste.

Alternative filling for lemon meringue pie

you will need:

1 large can condensed milk	2 oz. sugar
juice and grated rind 1 large lemon	2 level teaspoons cream of tartar
2 eggs	

1 Mix the condensed milk, lemon juice and rind, egg yolks and cream of tartar.
2 Use to fill an 8–9-inch pastry case or 14–16 tartlet cases.
3 Cover with meringue made with 2 egg whites and 4 oz. sugar.

Glacé icing

you will need:

8 oz. icing sugar	flavouring and colouring as liked
2–3 tablespoons warm water	

1 Sieve the icing sugar into a bowl, using a wooden spoon to press sugar through sieve, if necessary.

Add water gradually, beating well until icing is smooth and glossy, and of a good coating consistency, i.e. will coat the back of a spoon. Add flavouring and colouring, and blend it well into the mixture.

If icing is required only for the top of the cake, it should be slightly thicker so that it can be spread out smoothly and be kept to the edge.

Lemon or orange glacé icing

Make as above, using 2 tablespoons lemon or orange juice instead of water, and add 2–3 drops orange or lemon colouring.

Coffee glacé icing

Make as above, reducing the amount of water by 2 teaspoons, and using 2 teaspoons coffee essence.

Chocolate glacé icing

Melt 2 oz. plain chocolate in a small bowl over a pan of hot water. Blend in 4 oz. sieved icing sugar and 1 tablespoon water. For extra gloss, add 2–3 drops oil.

Chocolate icing

Break a 4 oz. bar of chocolate into a small bowl over a pan of hot water. Heat gently until the chocolate has melted, taking care that the water does not boil. Add a few drops of water and olive oil, if liked, to give a thin glossy coating icing.

Chocolate frosting

Melt 6 oz. plain chocolate in a basin over hot water. Stir in 12 oz. sieved icing sugar and blend in 6 tablespoons evaporated milk. Beat until smooth. Allow to cool, beat again and spread over cake or cakes as liked.

Feather icing

Cover cake with glacé icing. Before the icing sets, pipe lines (with a writing pipe) of icing in a contrasting colour across the cake.

Run a knife across the cake in the opposite direction, cutting through the lines of icing at right angles.

Work quickly, using a light pressure on the knife, making the 'lines' about $\frac{1}{2}$ inch apart.

Milky bar icing

Melt 1 large Milky bar and 2 tablespoons water together in a bowl over hot water.
For coating—add 4 oz. sieved icing sugar.
For spreading—add 6 oz. sieved icing sugar
For piping—add 7 oz. sieved icing sugar
For rolling out—add 9 oz. sieved icing sugar
Colour with vegetable colourings to suit the cake.

Vienna icing

you will need:

6 oz. icing sugar	2 tablespoons sherry
2 oz. butter	colouring (optional)

1 Sieve the icing sugar.
2 Beat butter until soft and gradually work in the icing sugar.
3 Add the sherry and continue beating until the icing is smooth.
4 Add colouring, if liked.

Orange Vienna icing

Make as above, adding 1 level teaspoon grated orange rind.

Chocolate Vienna icing

Make as above, replacing 1 tablespoon icing sugar with one of cocoa.

American frosting

you will need:

1 lb. loaf sugar	pinch cream of tartar
$\frac{1}{4}$ pint water	2 egg whites

1 Dissolve the sugar in the water, add a pinch of cream of tartar and boil rapidly until mixture reaches temperature of 240°F.
2 Whisk the egg whites until stiff.
3 Pour sugar syrup in a thin stream on to the egg whites and continue whisking until mixture thickens sufficiently to hold in peaks.
4 Spread quickly over the cake.

Seven-minute frosting

you will need:

2 egg whites	4 tablespoons water
12 oz. castor sugar	large pinch cream of tartar
pinch salt	colouring (optional)

1 Put all the ingredients in a bowl and whisk lightly.
2 Place bowl over hot water and continue whisking until mixture thickens sufficiently to hold in peaks.
3 Tint with a few drops of colouring, if liked.

Chocolate frosting

you will need:

4 oz. plain chocolate	2 egg yolks
½ oz. butter	4 tablespoons milk
4 oz. icing sugar, sieved	½ teaspoon vanilla essence

1 Melt chocolate in a bowl over hot water.
2 Add butter, beat in remaining ingredients.
3 Whisk mixture until it will thickly coat the back of a spoon.
4 Swirl over cake.

Creamy frosting

you will need:

1 lb. icing sugar	2 tablespoons water
pinch salt	1 egg white
4 oz. butter	colouring (optional)
1 teaspoon vanilla essence	

1 Sieve the icing sugar and salt.
2 Beat the butter until really soft, and gradually work in ⅓ of the sugar.
3 Add the vanilla essence and water and beat until well blended.
4 Beat in half the remaining sugar, then the egg white.
5 Gradually beat in the remaining sugar until the icing is the consistency required. If the icing is difficult to beat at any stage, add a little lemon juice or water.
6 Add colouring, if liked.

Caramel frosting

you will need:

6 oz. icing sugar	1½ tablespoons blended
3 oz. soft brown sugar	vegetable oil
1½–2 tablespoons milk	

1 Sieve the sugars together.
2 Blend in the oil and milk to give a spreading consistency, and beat well.

Vanilla frosting

you will need:

5 oz. icing sugar	1 tablespoon milk
1½ tablespoons blended	3–4 drops vanilla essence
vegetable oil	

1 Sieve the icing sugar.
2 Blend in the oil, milk and vanilla essence, and beat well.

Marshmallow frosting

you will need:

4 oz. marshmallows (about	2 egg whites
20 pink or white)	1 oz. sugar
2 tablespoons milk	

1 Melt the marshmallows slowly in the milk and leave to cool, stirring occasionally.
2 Beat the egg whites and sugar till stiff and peaky.
3 Fold into marshmallow mixture, and leave to set a little before using.

Honey frosting

Put 2 oz. honey, 8 oz. castor sugar, 2 egg whites and a pinch of salt in a bowl over boiling water. Add a few drops of lemon juice, if liked. Whisk thoroughly over boiling water until frosting is stiff enough to stand in peaks —about 6 minutes. Remove from heat and whisk for 1 minute more.

Apricot almond filling

Blend 2 tablespoons ground almonds with 2 tablespoons apricot jam. Add a few drops almond essence. Fold in 1 tablespoon double cream, whisked until thick.

Spicy frosting

you will need:

1 lb. icing sugar	3 tablespoons butter
½ level teaspoon powdered	3 tablespoons hot black
cinnamon	coffee
pinch ground cloves	½ teaspoon vanilla essence

1 Sieve the icing sugar and spices into a bowl.
2 Beat in the butter, coffee and vanilla essence.
3 Continue beating until mixture is of a spreading consistency.
4 This quantity is sufficient to cover the top and sides of an 8-inch cake.

Simple fondant icing

you will need:

1 lb. icing sugar	1 egg white
2 oz. glucose	flavouring and colouring

1 Sieve the icing sugar into a bowl.
2 Make a well in the centre. Add the glucose, dissolved in a little water, the egg white and flavouring, and colouring, if liked.
3 Beat well. Draw the icing sugar into the centre; continue beating until the mixture forms a stiff paste.
4 Turn out on to a surface dusted with icing sugar. Knead until smooth and pliable.

Apricot glaze

you will need:

4 tablespoons apricot jam   lemon juice (optional)
2 tablespoons water

1 Sieve the apricot jam into a small pan.
2 Add the water and bring to the boil.
3 Add lemon juice to taste, if liked.
  Use to glaze small cakes and for brushing cakes before applying almond paste.

Blanched almonds

Put into cold water. Bring almost to boiling point. Pour away the hot water and cover the almonds with cold water. Rub in a soft cloth and 'pinch' off the skins. Almonds for decoration are usually split lengthwise and used rounded side up. To give them a good shine, brush with egg white and dry off in the oven.

Toasted almonds

Blanch the almonds. Spread on a baking sheet and place in a moderate oven or under the grill until golden. Turn frequently. When cold, store in a jar until required.

Almonds may be tossed in a little melted butter before 'browning'. Drain well on kitchen paper, but do not store.

Almond paste

you will need:

6 oz. icing sugar   2 or 3 drops almond
12 oz. ground almonds   essence
6 oz. castor sugar   2 eggs

1 Sieve the icing sugar.
2 Mix the ground almonds, castor and icing sugar together.
3 Add the essence and eggs.
4 Knead until well mixed and smooth.

To cover a cake with almond paste

1 Trim the cake, if necessary, making the top flat. Brush off any crumbs.
2 Brush the top of the cake with warmed apricot jam.
3 Cut almond paste in half, roll out on a surface sprinkled with castor sugar into a round $\frac{1}{4}$-inch thick, the same size as the top of the cake.

4 Turn the cake upside down. Place on the round of almond paste and press down firmly. Trim the edge of the almond paste, if necessary. Turn cake upright again.
5 Measure the sides of the cake. Roll out the remaining paste into a strip of this length and width. Brush the strip of almond paste with warmed apricot jam.
6 Press the strip in position against the side of the cake, making a neat join. Roll a jam jar firmly over the top and around the sides of the cake. The strip of paste may be cut in one or two pieces for easier handling.
7 Allow the almond paste to dry out for 2–3 days in a cool place before icing the cake.

Guide to amount of almond paste and royal icing required for covering rich fruit cakes

Size of Cake

7-inch round	$1\frac{1}{4}$ lb. almond paste and royal icing
7-inch square	$1\frac{1}{2}$ lb. almond paste and royal icing
8-inch round	$1\frac{3}{4}$ lb. almond paste and royal icing
8-inch square	2 lb. almond paste and royal icing
9-inch round	2 lb. almond paste and royal icing
9-inch square	$2\frac{1}{4}$ lb. almond paste and royal icing

Royal icing

you will need:

1 lb. icing sugar   1 teaspoon lemon juice
2 egg whites $\frac{1}{2}$ teaspoon glycerine

1 Leave the egg whites in a cold place overnight.
2 Sieve the icing sugar.
3 Whisk the egg whites until frothy.
4 Beat in half the icing sugar, add the lemon juice and glycerine.
5 Continue beating in the sugar, until the icing can be drawn into stiff peaks.
6 Scrape the icing down from the sides of the bowl. Cover with a damp cloth and use as required.

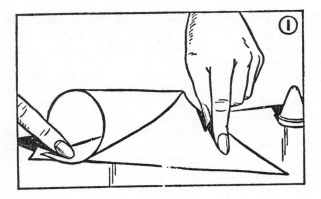

To pipe icing

Have ready an icing pipe and forcing pipe. The forcing bag may be bought (nylon or fabric) or it may be made with greaseproof paper as directed below. Choose a writing pipe for making lines, dots, scalloped edges and words. Use a star pipe for making rosettes, ropes or coils, or for zig-zag lines, and a shell pipe for a firm, well-defined edge.

To pipe icing on a cake, work with the pipe held close to the surface of the cake, but not touching it. Work from the centre of the top outwards.

If several pipes are used in the design or more than one colour of icing, have several bags ready with pipes in position before starting to decorate the cake.

To make a forcing bag

1 Cut a 10-inch square of greaseproof paper diagonally across to form two triangles. Shape each triangle into a cone as illustrated.

2 Bring the three points together and hold firmly between thumb and forefinger.

3 Secure the three points together with a paper clip or by folding the paper over several times.

4 Cut off a small piece, about $\frac{1}{2}$ inch from the point of the cone and drop in the icing pipe. About $\frac{1}{2}$ inch of the pipe should protrude.

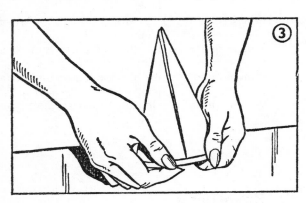

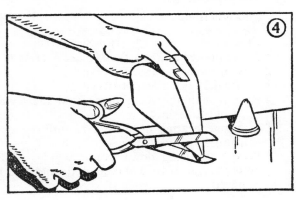

Fondant icing

you will need:

2 lb. loaf or granulated sugar
$\frac{1}{2}$ pint water

4 oz. glucose or $\frac{1}{2}$ teaspoon cream of tartar

1 Dissolve the sugar in the water over a low heat.

2 Add the glucose or cream of tartar, bring to the boil quickly.

3 Continue boiling until a temperature of 240°F. is reached.

4 Pour on to a marble slab, brushed with oil or water and leave to cool until a skin begins to form round the edge.

5 Work the icing syrup backwards and forwards with a spatula or palette knife until it becomes firm and opaque. Keep the mixture together as much as possible.

6 Knead the icing by hand until of an even texture throughout.

7 Use at once or wrap in greaseproof paper and store in a cool place until required.
8 To use after storing, heat in a basin over a pan of hot water, stirring until the consistency of thick cream. Allow to cool.

If a slab is not available, the icing can be 'worked' in a large bowl.

Fondant Icing may be used as a foundation for royal or glacé icing in place of almond paste. When used in this way it may be flavoured with almond essence and it may also be mixed with desiccated coconut. It can also be used for coating rich cakes with or without fruit.

Scraps of fondant icing can be kept and used to make decorations for iced cakes, flowers and fruit, etc.

To cover a cake with fondant icing

Have the cake covered with almond paste a few days beforehand to allow the paste to dry out.

1 Brush the surface of almond paste with egg white.
2 Dust rolling pin and working surface with sieved icing sugar.
3 Roll the fondant out, at least $\frac{1}{4}$ inch thick. Lift on to the cake, using the rolling pin.
4 Dust the palms of the hands with sieved icing sugar and smooth the icing over the top of the cake, working it down the sides and making sure that the corners are neat.
5 Trim off the uneven icing from the base of the cake.
6 Have cake board ready, also some royal icing made up, if the cake is to be stuck into position.
7 Lift cake with two fish slices or palette knives and place on the board.

If the cake is to be 'stuck' on to the board, roughly spread royal icing over the board before placing the cake in position.

Special-occasion Cakes

Every family celebration calls for a special cake, iced and decorated in traditional style. The cake is usually made from a rich fruit mixture, covered with almond paste and royal icing. It is important to make the cake several weeks before it is required to allow it time to mature. Once the almond paste has been applied, the cake should be stored in a cool, dry place to allow the paste to dry out. After the cake has been covered with icing, it may be decorated by piping with royal icing. Piping requires a good deal of practice to get a really good finish, so keep the design simple. If you don't feel able to cope with this, use a little imagination and you will find that you can achieve an attractive finish with very little difficulty. Here are two ideas to start you off: stick a rosette of ribbon, the kind you buy ready-made-up for gift wrapping, in the centre of the cake with a dab of icing. Tuck a few sprigs of holly, heather or fresh flowers into the loops of ribbon; or make a cluster of tiny Christmas tree baubles, fastening them together with pipe cleaners pushed through the wire loops. Place in the centre of the cake, finish with a bow of scarlet ribbon.

White Christmas cake

cooking time   2½–3 hours

you will need:

12 oz. flour	6 oz. stem ginger, drained
pinch salt	and chopped
1 level teaspoon baking	6 oz. glacé pineapple,
powder	chopped
8 oz. butter	4 oz. candied peel, chopped
8 oz. castor sugar	4 oz. walnuts, chopped
4 large eggs	grated rind 1 lemon
juice ½ lemon	

1 Grease and line an 8-inch round cake tin.
2 Sieve flour, salt and baking powder.
3 Cream butter and sugar until light and fluffy.
4 Beat in the eggs gradually.
5 Fold in the flour.
6 Add the fruit, nuts, rind and juice. Mix gently.
7 Turn mixture into cake tin. Bake at 325°F.—Mark 3, covering cake with paper during last hour.
8 Remove cake from tin, strip off paper, and leave cake on a wire tray until cold.
9 Cover cake with almond paste (see page 37) and royal icing (see page 37).

Starlight cake

cooking time 5–5½ hours

you will need:

8 oz. flour	finely grated rind 1
4 oz. fine semolina	medium orange
1 level teaspoon mixed	8 oz. each currants
spice	and sultanas, washed
½ level teaspoon each	and dried
nutmeg and cinnamon	4 oz. seedless raisins,
1 tablespoon instant coffee	washed and dried
powder	4 oz. dates, finely chopped
pinch salt	4 oz. glacé cherries,
8 oz. butter or margarine	quartered
8 oz. soft brown sugar	2 oz. chopped mixed peel
4 large eggs	2 oz. walnuts or blanched
2 level tablespoons golden	almonds, finely chopped
syrup	

1 Grease and line an 8–9 inch round cake tin.
2 Sieve the dry ingredients together.
3 Cream the fat and sugar until light and fluffy.
4 Add the eggs, one at a time, beating thoroughly after each addition.
5 Stir in the syrup, half the dry ingredients, orange rind and all the fruit and nuts. Mix thoroughly.
6 Stir in the remaining flour, then turn mixture into the prepared tin.
7 Bake in the centre of a cool oven 290°F.— Mark 1.
8 Leave in the tin for at least half an hour, then turn out on to a wire tray and remove the paper.

To decorate starlight cake

1 Cover cake with almond paste (see page 37), allow to dry out.
2 Put cake on to a board, then spread fairly thickly with royal icing (see page 37). Smooth top with a palette knife dipped in hot water and 'rough up' the sides.
3 Finish top and lower edges with piped rosettes of icing, then decorate cake with glittering stars.

To make stars

Cut small star shapes from thin cardboard, brush with glue then sprinkle with granulated sugar. Alternatively, cut shapes from almond paste, brush with egg white and sprinkle with granulated sugar.

Rose and star or anniversary cake

1 Cover an 8-inch round cake with white royal or fondant icing (see pages 37–38). Place on a board and leave to dry.
2 Draw a 6-pointed star on thin card or stiff paper. Cut out shape and place in the centre of the cake.
3 Prick round the outline with a needle or a very fine skewer, then remove the shape.
4 Using a No. 1 writing tube and royal icing, pipe the shape of the star, following the 'pricked' outline.
5 Fill the star with pastel tinted glacé icing (see page 34), or royal icing thinned with lemon juice. Use a fine brush or the tip of a knife to ease the icing into the points. Leave to dry.
6 Make a cluster of small roses and leaves (bought or made of icing or almond paste— see page 37) in the centre of the star, sticking them into position with a little royal icing.
7 Pipe a shell edge using a No. 12 nozzle and white royal icing around the base of the cake where it joins the board. Decorate with small sprays of roses and leaves, working from the shell edge up the sides of the cake.

Star Christmas cake

Prepare the cake as above. Stud the star outline with silver balls or fill the star with silver balls. Fix a candle in a holder in the centre of the star and decorate with red ribbon and holly. Pipe shell edge around the base, stud with silver balls and arrange holly leaves about 2 inches apart on the shell edge.

Birthday cake for a six-year-old

Prepare cake as for a star cake. Outline six small stars, about 1½ inches in size, on the top of the cake. Fill with coloured icing or silver balls and place a small candle in the centre of each star. Tie a broad band of ribbon round the cake, fasten with a bow or use a cake frill to finish off.

Birthday or Christmas cake

cooking time 4½–5 hours

you will need:

8 oz. plain flour	8 oz. currants
pinch salt	8 oz. raisins
½ teaspoon spice	3 oz. glacé cherries
½ teaspoon nutmeg	3 oz. candied peel
8 oz. butter	2 oz. blanched almonds
8 oz. brown sugar	3 tablespoons lemon juice
4 eggs	grated rind 1 lemon
8 oz. sultanas	3–4 tablespoons brandy
	(optional)

1 Grease and line a 7-inch square or 8-inch round tin with a double thickness of greased greaseproof paper.
2 Sieve flour, salt and spices.
3 Cream the butter and sugar together until light and fluffy. Beat the eggs into the creamed mixture.
4 Fold in the sieved flour. Add lemon juice and rind.
5 Stir in the prepared fruit and nuts, mix all well together and put into tin.

40

6 Bake in a slow oven, at 290°F.—Mark 1. Allow cake to cool before removing from tin.

7 Prick the bottom of the cake, spoon brandy over it and allow to soak in. When cold, wrap in greaseproof or foil and store in an airtight tin until required.

8 Cover with almond paste (see page 37).

9 Coat with royal icing (see page 37) and decorate.

Eggless Christmas cake

cooking time   3 hours

you will need:

10 oz. flour	10 oz. margarine
pinch salt	1 large can sweetened
¾ level teaspoon	condensed milk
bicarbonate of soda	8 oz. currants
½ pint water	8 oz. sultanas
4 oz. mixed peel, chopped	2 oz. glacé cherries
4 oz. blanched almonds	finely grated rind 1 orange
	and 2 lemons

1 Grease and line either an 8-inch square or a 7–8-inch round cake tin.

2 Chop the cherries and almonds.

3 Put with the water, margarine, fruit, chopped peel, grated rinds and condensed milk into a saucepan.

4 Bring to the boil, stirring all the time. Lower the heat and simmer for 3 minutes.

5 Remove from the heat and allow to cool.

6 Sieve flour and salt into a mixing bowl.

7 Add the bicarbonate of soda to the cooled fruit mixture and stir quickly.

8 Add to the flour mixture and mix quickly together.

9 Put into the prepared tin and spread evenly.

10 Bake on the middle shelf at 310°F.—Mark 2.

11 Cool for at least 5 minutes in the tin, then turn out on a wire tray until cold.

12 If liked, this mixture may be baked in an oblong tin, 14 × 19 inches, or half the mixture may be used and baked in a 6-inch tin. Bake for 2 hours. Ice and decorate as described on pages 37–38.

The cake mixture may also be steamed or boiled for 5 hours to give an economical Christmas pudding.

Christmas cake (made with oil)

cooking time   2½–3 hours

you will need:

¼ pint corn oil	4 oz. currants
2 eggs	4 oz. sultanas
6 oz. soft brown sugar	4 oz. raisins
10 oz. flour	2 oz. candied peel,
1½ level teaspoons baking	chopped
powder	2 oz. blanched almonds,
pinch salt	chopped
2 tablespoons milk	2 oz. glacé cherries

1 Grease and line a 7-inch round cake tin.

2 Clean and dry the fruit, then dredge with a little of the flour.

3 Beat the corn oil, eggs and sugar well together in a bowl.

4 Mix in the remainder of the flour sieved with the baking powder and salt.

5 Add the milk.

6 Finally, add the fruit, stir well and turn into the prepared tin.

7 Bake in a slow oven 310°F.—Mark 2.

8 Allow to cool in the tin for 10 minutes before turning on to a wire tray. Ice and decorate as described on pages 37–38.

Rich fruit cake (suitable for Christmas or 21st birthday cake)

cooking time   4–4½ hours

you will need:

8 oz. soft brown sugar	1 lb. currants
8 oz. butter	8 oz. raisins
5 eggs	8 oz. sultanas
10 oz. flour	4 oz. glacé cherries,
½ oz. mixed spice	chopped
¾ teaspoon almond essence	4 oz. chopped mixed peel
¾ teaspoon lemon essence	rum, brandy, or cherry
1 tablespoon black treacle	brandy for steeping the
marmalade	fruit and for pouring over
	the cake

1 Grease and line a 9-inch cake tin. Tie folded brown paper or newspaper round the outside of the tin.

2 Put all the fruit into a bowl and pour a wine-glass of spirit over it. Leave overnight.

3 Sieve the flour and spice.

4 Cream the fat and sugar until light and fluffy. Add the essence, and the treacle or marmalade.

5 Gradually beat in the eggs.

6 Lightly fold in half the flour. Mix the remaining flour with the fruit. Stir into the cake mixture.

7 Turn mixture into the tin, make a shallow hollow in the centre.

8 Place a pad of newspaper in the oven on the middle shelf. Bake the cake on this at 335°F.—Mark 3, for 1 hour. Reduce to 310°F.—Mark 2, for the next hour, then reduce to 290°F.—Mark 1, for the remaining cooking time. Cover the cake with paper if it becomes too brown.

9 Turn the cake on to a wire tray. Remove the paper. Prick the bottom of the cake, spoon brandy over it and allow to soak in.

10 When the cake is cold, wrap it in foil or grease-proof paper and store until required.

Make the cake 6–8 weeks before it is required. Ice as described on pages 37–38.

Simnel cake

cooking time   3 hours

you will need:

8 oz. flour	6 oz. butter
pinch salt	6 oz. sugar
1 teaspoon grated nutmeg	3 eggs
1 teaspoon cinnamon	milk to mix
3 oz. chopped mixed peel	beaten egg for glazing
12 oz. currants	almond paste
4 oz. sultanas	apricot jam

1 Make almond paste using 8 oz. ground almonds (see page 37).
2 Grease and line an 8-inch cake tin.
3 Sieve flour, salt and spices.
4 Cream the butter and sugar.
5 Beat in the eggs gradually.
6 Fold in the sieved flour.
7 Stir in the fruit lightly, adding a little milk if necessary to make a soft dropping consistency.
8 Put half the mixture into the tin, smooth top with a knife.
9 Roll $\frac{1}{3}$ of the almond paste into a round the size of the tin.
10 Place the round of almond paste into the cake tin and press lightly into position and cover with remaining cake mixture.
11 Bake in a slow oven 310°F.—Mark 2. Cool on a wire tray.
12 Roll out half remaining almond paste into a round to cover the top of the cake. Make 11 small balls with remaining paste.
13 Brush the top of the cake with warmed apricot jam. Press the round of almond paste firmly in place. Arrange the balls round the edge, sticking in place with a little beaten egg. Brown in a hot oven or under the grill.
14 Decorate the finished cake with primroses, real or artificial, or a large bow of yellow ribbon.

Easter egg cake

Cover a shallow round fruit cake with almond paste (see page 37). Rough up the sides with a fork to resemble a bird's nest. Brush all over with beaten egg and brown quickly in a hot oven. Decorate the top of the cake with small chocolate or almond paste eggs wrapped in silver paper and a fluffy chicken.

Easter flower cake

Cover a round fruit cake with almond paste (see page 37). Score the top in squares or diamonds with a sharp pointed knife. Brush with beaten egg and brown under a hot grill. Decorate with a small posy of spring flowers made of coloured almond paste, or use fresh or artificial flowers.

Arrange a bow of ribbon on the 'stalks' of the flowers and allow the ends to trail over the top of the cake.

Wedding cake

cooking time $3\frac{3}{4}$—$6\frac{3}{4}$ hours

you will need:

$1\frac{1}{2}$ lb. currants	10 oz. ground almonds
$1\frac{1}{2}$ lb. sultanas	$1\frac{1}{2}$ lb. flour
$1\frac{1}{4}$ lb. raisins	$\frac{1}{4}$ teaspoon salt
10 oz. cherries	$2\frac{1}{2}$ teaspoons nutmeg
10 oz. peel	$2\frac{1}{2}$ teaspoons mixed spice
$1\frac{1}{2}$ lb. butter	$2\frac{1}{2}$ teaspoons cinnamon
$1\frac{1}{2}$ lb. sugar	brandy
2 lemons	10 lb. almond paste (see
12 eggs	page 37)
	10 lb. icing sugar

1 Grease three round tins 10, 8 and 6 inches, and line each with a double thickness of greased greaseproof paper.
2 Prepare the fruit. Chop the cherries and peel.
3 Sieve flour, salt and spices into a large bowl (clean washing-up bowl may be used).
4 Mix all the prepared fruit with the sieved flour.
5 Grate the lemon rind very finely.
6 Cream the butter and sugar until white and shiny.
7 Beat in the lemon rind.
8 Beat in the eggs, one at a time, adding a little of the ground almonds after each egg.
9 Lightly stir in the fruit and flour mixture and any remaining almonds.
10 Divide the mixture between the three tins and bake in a slow oven 290°F.—Mark 1. Allow $3\frac{3}{4}$–4 hours for the 6-inch tin, $4\frac{1}{2}$–$4\frac{3}{4}$ for the 8-inch tin, and $6\frac{1}{4}$–$6\frac{3}{4}$ for the 10-inch tin.
11 Remove the cakes from the oven as each is cooked and allow to cool in the tin for at least 10 minutes. Turn on a wire tray, strip off the greaseproof paper.
12 Prick the bottom of each cake with a fine skewer or needle. Pour 3–4 tablespoons brandy over each and leave to soak in.
13 When the cakes are completely cold, wrap each in foil and store in a cool dry place for at least 3 weeks or up to 3 months.

If preferred, the cake may be made in two stages. Use half the quantity for the large tin and divide the remaining mixture between the two smaller tins. The whole mixture may be prepared and cooked separately. Leave the cakes in a cool place until ready to go into the oven.

Half this mixture may be used to make a 10-inch round or a 9-inch square cake suitable for a 21st birthday cake.

Icing and decorating the Wedding cake

1 Brush each cake with apricot glaze (see page 37). Cover with almond paste (see page 37) and leave to dry out for at least one week before applying the first coat of icing.
2 Coat each cake with stiff royal icing (see page 37) and leave to harden for at least 2 days, making sure it is protected from dust.
3 Coat the cakes a second time, making the royal icing slightly thinner (so that it will coat the back of a spoon).
4 When the cakes are dry, fix each to a board, using a generous amount of royal icing. Use a board at least 1 inch larger than the iced cake.
5 Using a round cutter, lightly mark semi-circles round the edge of each cake, about 1 inch down from the top of the cake, making a scalloped-edge effect.
6 Pipe the scallop round each cake, using royal icing and a writing tube. Leave to dry.
7 Using a No. 12 nozzle, pipe a raised edge round the top and base of each cake. Leave to dry.
8 When the cake is required, place one tier on top of the other. Decorate with real, home-made or bought flowers, silver leaves and ribbon.
If preferred the tiers may be supported by pillars. Use four 3-inch pillars on the bottom tier to support the 8-inch cake and four 4-inch pillars to support the 6-inch cake.
The flowers may be arranged in a silver vase on the top tier if preferred.

Traditional plum cake

cooking time   6–6½ hours

you will need:

1 lb. seeded raisins	8 oz. butter or margarine
1 lb. sultanas	4 oz. soft brown sugar
1 lb. currants	4 level tablespoons golden
4 oz. mixed peel	syrup
9 oz. flour	finely grated rind 2 lemons
pinch salt	4 eggs
1 heaped teaspoon mixed	2 oz. ground almonds
spice	1 tablespoon sherry
1 rounded teaspoon grated	
nutmeg	

1 Grease and line a 9-inch square tin.
2 Wash and dry fruit, if necessary, and chop peel.
3 Sieve flour, salt and spices.
4 Cream fat, sugar and syrup, adding the lemon rind.
5 Beat in the eggs, one at a time, adding the ground almonds gradually, alternately with the eggs.
6 Mix flour and fruit, and lightly stir in to the creamed mixture, adding the sherry.

7 Spread the mixture in the tin, and bake in a slow oven 290°F.—Mark 1.
8 Allow cake to cool in the tin for ½ hour, then turn on to a wire tray and leave until cold.

Hallowe'en cake

cooking time   30 minutes

you will need:

8 oz. self-raising flour	5 oz. castor sugar
2 level tablespoons cocoa	2 level tablespoons golden
½ level teaspoon nutmeg	syrup
½ level teaspoon mixed	3 eggs
spice	3 oz. sultanas
1 level teaspoon cinnamon	½ teaspoon vanilla essence
6 oz. butter or margarine	4 tablespoons milk

1 Grease two 8-inch sandwich tins.
2 Sieve together the flour, cocoa and spices.
3 Cream the fat and sugar until light and fluffy, and add the essence.
4 Beat in the syrup (warmed slightly, if liked) and the eggs.
5 Fold in the flour, adding milk to make a soft mixture.
6 Divide between the two tins. Bake at 375°F.—Mark 5.
7 Turn on to a wire tray and leave until cold.
8 Sandwich together with frosting and coat with frosting. Sprinkle thickly with coarsely grated plain chocolate.

Frosting
you will need:

10 oz. icing sugar	3 drops each vanilla and
5 oz. butter	almond essence
	1 dessertspoon milk

1 Sieve the icing sugar.
2 Beat the butter until soft, beat in sugar and essence. Continue beating until very light and fluffy.
3 Beat in milk.

Basket of flowers cake

Brush the outside of an 8-inch sandwich cake 3–4 inches deep with warm apricot jam. Cover sides of cake with thinly rolled almond paste (see page 37). Mark with a fork or a skewer to suggest the weave of a basket. Spread the top of the cake with butter cream, chocolate or lemon flavoured (see page 33). Fill the top of the basket with small coloured flowers made in almond paste. Make a short handle from almond paste by plaiting three thin strips of paste and fixing these in place with butter cream. Tie a bow of ribbon in the centre of the handle and allow the end of the ribbon to hang down.

Posy of flowers cake

Prepare the cake as above, coating the top with thick glacé icing (see page 34) instead of butter cream. When the icing has set, place a doily, trimmed to fit, on the top of the cake. Fill the centre of the doily with flowers made from almond paste (see page 37), using cotton wool in the centre to build up the posy. Small fresh or plastic flowers may be used. These can be easily removed by lifting the doily off the top of the cake.

Birthday cake for a little girl

Bake a light fruit, cherry or madeira cake in a greased ovenproof basin, 5–6 inches diameter at the widest part. Cover with almond paste (see page 37), if liked, when the cake is cold.

1 Fix the cake on to a cake board. Coat with royal icing or frosting (see pages 37 and 43), swirling the icing to give a frilled or pannier effect.
2 Fix a china 'crinoline lady's head and top half of her body' (the kind used for making a tea cosy) in the centre of the cake.
3 Tie a narrow ribbon round the 'doll's' waist making a bow at the back, with the ends of the ribbon trailing down the skirt. Decorate the dress with matching bows of ribbon and sprays of small flowers.

Birthday book cake

Bake a light fruit, cherry or madeira cake in an oblong tin, approximately 11 by 7½ by 1½ inches.

1 Place cake on a board about 1 inch larger all round than the cake.
2 Cut a V-shaped wedge down the centre of the cake (cutting across the cake, not lengthways), so that it represents an open book.
3 Trim the outside edges of the cake, cutting them so they slope in slightly from the board, to represent the pages.
4 Cover the cake with fondant icing (about 1½ lb.) (see pages 38), allowing it to extend ¼ inch all round the base of the cake, to represent the edges of the pages. Leave to dry.
5 Mark the 'sloped' edges with the prongs of a fork, to represent the leaves of the book. Leave to dry.
6 With a fine brush and edible colouring, paint the fondant icing where it meets the board as the cover of the book.

7 Pipe a birthday greeting across the top of the cake (using coloured royal icing (see page 37) and a writing tube).
8 Fix a piece of ribbon down the centre of the cake as a book mark.

Christening cake

Bake a light fruit, cherry or madeira cake in an oblong tin, approximately 8 x 5 inches.

1 Cover with white fondant icing (see page 38), fix on to a cake board and leave to dry.
2 Pipe edges with royal icing (see page 37), tinted to a pastel shade, to represent basket weave.
3 Roll out a piece of fondant icing into an oblong about ⅔ the size of the top of the cake. Mark into a diamond pattern with a pointed knife. This is to represent a quilt.
4 Form a small piece of fondant icing into a pillow and fix this into position in the centre of one end of the cake. Place the quilt into position. Tuck a very small doll under the quilt with just the head showing on the pillow.
5 Pipe the top and bottom end of the cot with royal icing, using a small shell pipe, and decorate with tiny bows of pink or blue baby ribbon.
6 A small frill of net may be fastened round the edge of the cot, if liked.

Christmas garland

you will need:

1 sponge cake baked in an 8-inch round or ring tin	green colouring
2 large Milky bars	approximately 12 oz. icing sugar
4 tablespoons water	holly leaves, bells or gold and silver leaves
glacé cherries	

1 Melt the Milky bars with water in a bowl over hot water.
2 Remove from the heat and add the colouring.
3 Beat in the sieved icing sugar and pour over the cake.
4 Decorate with holly leaves round the top and small pieces of glacé cherry.
5 Place on a silver cake board.
6 Decorate with more holly leaves and silver bells.

Santa Claus cake

you will need:

1 sponge cake baked in a tin approximately 9 × 14 inches	4 tablespoons water
sieved jam	approximately 1 lb. 4 oz. icing sugar, sieved
2 large Milky bars	red and yellow colouring

1 Cut a 5-inch circle from the sponge and two 4-inch triangles.

2 Place the circle on a cake board. Place one triangle at an angle at the top for a hat, and one straight at the base for a beard, cutting each to fit round the circle.

3 Brush the surfaces with jam and press into place.

4 Melt the Milky bars with the water in a bowl over a pan of hot water, stirring continuously.

5 Remove from the heat and divide in half. Colour one half red, and the other yellow.

6 Beat about 9 oz. icing sugar into each half.

7 Roll out a triangle in red on a surface dusted with icing sugar. Place over the top triangle.

8 Place a walnut-sized ball in yellow on top of the hat for a top-knot.

9 Fix two yellow ovals for eyes and dot with red in the centre.

10 Make a nose-shape and a handlebar moustache in yellow and attach on to the face.

11 Roll out a triangle in yellow for the beard and fix on to the lower triangle.

Igloo cake

you will need:

1 sponge or fruit cake baked in a 7-inch fireproof basin	sieved apricot jam
	2 large Milky bars
	4 tablespoons water
8 oz. almond paste (see page 37)	5 oz. icing sugar, sieved

1 Place the cake flat side down and cut an arch-shaped piece out for the door.

2 Brush the cake all over with jam.

3 Shape a small piece of almond paste for the dome-shaped top and attach it to the cake.

4 Roll out the remaining almond paste and use to cover the cake.

5 Melt the Milky bars and water together in a basin over a pan of hot water.

6 Remove from the heat and beat in the icing sugar.

7 Pour the icing over the igloo.

8 Mark in squares all over with the back of a knife.

9 Sprinkle lightly with icing sugar.

10 Put the igloo on to a round 9-inch silver cake board.

11 Decorate with toy eskimos and holly.

Cracker cake

Have a Swiss roll prepared and about 1½ lb. fondant icing (see page 36) or Milky bar icing (see previous recipe).

1 Roll the icing out into an oblong 2 inches longer than the cake.

2 Brush the cake with warm apricot jam and cover completely with icing.

3 Dust the palms of the hands with icing sugar and shape icing to represent a cracker. Snip the ends of the icing with kitchen scissors to make a fringe.

4 Fasten a bow of ribbon on to each end.

5 Pipe top with a simple design in coloured royal icing (see page 37).
Decorate with silver balls, holly, etc.

Miscellaneous Cakes

'Miscellaneous' cakes are those which do not quite conform to the basic methods of cake-making already described; but a book on cake-making would be incomplete without these family favourites.

Strawberry shortcake

cooking time   30–40 minutes

you will need:

8 oz. self-raising flour	1 egg yolk
good pinch salt	strawberries
½ oz. ground almonds	½ pint double cream
4½ oz. butter	sugar to taste
2 oz. sugar	

1 Sieve the flour and salt into a bowl, add the ground almonds, mix well.

2 Cream the fat and sugar and beat in the egg yolk.

3 Work in the flour by hand, knead well.

4 Divide the mixture into three. Roll into rounds a good ¼ inch thick.

5 Place each on a greased baking tray and bake in a moderate oven 350°F.—Mark 4, until golden.

6 Place on a wire tray until cold.

7 Sprinkle the strawberries with sugar to taste. Crush slightly with a fork, saving a few for decoration.

8 Whisk the cream until thick.

9 Mix ¾ of the cream with the crushed strawberries.

10 Sandwich the layers of shortcake with the strawberry and cream mixture, and decorate the top with cream and the whole strawberries.

Apple shortcake

Prepare shortcake as before. Peel, core and slice 1 lb. cooking apples. Stew the apples with 4 oz. sugar, ¼ teaspoon cinnamon, grated rind of 1 lemon and 2 oz. sultanas. When cool, sandwich the shortcakes with this filling. Decorate the top with whipped cream or dust with sugar.

This filling may also be used to make an apple meringue pie. Fill a cooked flan case with the apple, top with meringue and bake in a slow oven until the meringue is crisp.

Devil's food cake

cooking time   25–30 minutes

you will need:

6 oz. flour	4 tablespoons milk
2 level teaspoons baking powder	2 egg yolks
	4 egg whites
4 oz. margarine	butter cream (see page 33)
8 oz. sugar	glacé icing (see page 34)
4 oz. plain chocolate	or vanilla frosting (see page 36)

1 Grease and line two 8-inch sandwich tins.
2 Sieve the flour and baking powder.
3 Grate the chocolate into a bowl. Add the milk. Place the bowl over a pan of hot water. Heat gently until the chocolate is melted.
4 Cream the fat and sugar. Beat in the yolks and chocolate.
5 Fold in the flour.
6 Whisk the egg whites until stiff.
7 Stir lightly into the mixture and divide between the two tins.
8 Bake in a moderately hot oven 375°F.—Mark 5.
9 Cool on a wire tray.
10 Sandwich with butter cream and coat with white glacé icing or vanilla frosting.

Chocolate corner cake

cooking time   60–70 minutes

you will need:

8 oz. flour	2 eggs
2 teaspoons baking powder	good ¼ pint milk
1½ oz. cocoa	orange glacé icing (see page 35)
pinch salt	
4 oz. margarine	chocolate butter cream (see page 33)
6 oz. sugar	

1 Grease a square 7-inch tin and line the bottom with greased greaseproof paper.
2 Sieve flour, baking powder, cocoa and salt.
3 Cream the fat and sugar.
4 Separate the egg whites from the yolks.
5 Beat the yolks into the creamed mixture.
6 Fold in the flour, adding the milk gradually.

7 Whisk the egg whites until stiff and fold into the mixture.
8 Pour into the tin and bake in a moderately hot oven 375°F.—Mark 5.
9 Turn out on to a wire tray and leave to cool.
10 When cold, coat the cake with orange glacé icing. When this has set, pipe lines of chocolate butter cream across the cake diagonally.
11 Decorate with chocolate buttons, fixing these upright in the butter cream.

Battenburg cake

cooking time   25 minutes

you will need:

8 oz. flour	milk if necessary
1 teaspoon baking powder	½ oz. cocoa
8 oz. butter or margarine	8 oz. almond paste (see page 37)
8 oz. sugar	
3 eggs	apricot jam
vanilla essence	castor sugar

1 Grease and line two 1-lb. loaf tins.
2 Sieve flour and baking powder.
3 Cream fat and sugar, add 3–4 drops vanilla essence, beat in the eggs.
4 Fold in the flour, using a little milk if necessary to make a soft mixture.
5 Spread half this mixture into one tin.
6 Stir cocoa into the remaining mixture, using more milk, if necessary.
7 Spread this mixture into the second tin.
8 Bake in a moderately hot oven 375°F.—Mark 5.
9 Turn out on to a wire tray and leave until cold.
10 Trim cakes to an equal size and cut each in half lengthways.
11 Spread sides with jam (warmed if too stiff to spread) and stick pieces together, alternating the colours. Press firmly into shape.
12 Roll almond paste into an oblong on a sugared surface.
13 Place cake on almond paste, making sure that all outside surfaces are spread with jam.
14 Press two edges of almond paste together, brushing edges with egg white if necessary to seal. Turn cake over so that the join does not show.
15 Crimp top edges of almond paste lightly, score the top with a sharp knife in lines, squares or diamonds.
16 Dust with castor sugar. Wrap tightly in foil or greaseproof and leave in a cool place for 2–3 days before cutting.

Golden chiffon cake

cooking time   40–50 minutes

you will need:

6 oz. self-raising flour	2 eggs
pinch salt	grated rind 1 lemon
5 oz. castor sugar	4½ tablespoons orange juice
2½ oz. (5 tablespoons)	glacé icing (see page 34)
blended vegetable oil	

1 Grease an 8-inch cake tin and line it with greaseproof paper.
2 Sieve flour and salt into a basin. Add sugar and lemon rind.
3 Separate egg whites from yolks. Beat oil into the yolks and blend in the orange juice.
4 Make a well in the centre of the dry ingredients, pour in the yolk mixture. Beat with a wooden spoon for 2 minutes.
5 Whisk egg whites until stiff, fold into mixture.
6 Pour into prepared tin. Bake in a moderate oven 350°F.—Mark 4.
7 Cool on a wire tray until cold.
8 Coat top with glacé icing flavoured with the juice of the lemon. Decorate with crystallised orange and lemon slices.

Chocolate orange chiffon cake

Make as above, coat cake with chocolate glacé icing (see page 35). Decorate top with chopped pistachio nuts, if liked.

Strawberry angel cake

cooking time   1 hour

you will need:

4 oz. self-raising flour	5 tablespoons water
5 oz. castor sugar	½ teaspoon vanilla essence
½ teaspoon salt	grated rind ½ lemon
4 tablespoons corn oil	½ teaspoon cream of tartar
3 eggs	fresh strawberries
	whipped cream

1 Sift the flour, sugar and salt three times into a bowl.
2 Make a well in the centre and add the oil, egg yolks, water, vanilla essence and lemon rind.
3 Stir until smooth.
4 Sprinkle the cream of tartar over the egg whites, then beat the whites until very stiff.
5 Pour the batter on to the whites, one third at a time, and fold in gently. Do not stir.
6 Turn the mixture into an ungreased 7-inch tube cake tin.
7 Bake at 335°F.—Mark 3. Remove from the oven and cool upside-down in the tin for 30 minutes on a wire tray.
8 Turn out on a wire tray and leave until cold.
9 Fill with strawberries, decorate with cream.

Sherry frosted cakes

cooking time   15 minutes

you will need:

2 oz. plain flour	2 eggs
2 oz. fine semolina	¼ teaspoon vanilla essence
2 oz. ground almonds	¼ teaspoon almond essence
1 teaspoon baking powder	1 oz. chopped walnuts
pinch salt	sherry icing
4 oz. butter	glacé cherries or walnuts
2 oz. castor sugar	(optional)

1 Grease twenty small patty tins.
2 Sieve flour, semolina, almonds, baking powder and salt.
3 Melt butter and allow to cool slightly.
4 Stir in sugar, well beaten eggs and essence.
5 Stir in dry ingredients and chopped walnuts.
6 Two-thirds fill prepared tins.
7 Bake at 375°F.—Mark 5.
8 When cold, place a spoonful of sherry icing on top of each, swirling it with the back of the spoon, if liked.
9 Decorate with half a glacé cherry or walnut, if liked.

Sherry icing

Blend 4 heaped tablespoons icing sugar with 1½ tablespoons sherry.

Fruit and nut delights

Make cakes as above. Just before serving spread top with double cream, whipped until thick, and decorate with drained canned fruit. Sliced peaches or mandarin oranges are particularly good.

Truffle cakes

you will need:

4 oz. stale sponge cake	almond or rum essence
4 oz. castor sugar	(optional)
4 oz. ground almonds	chocolate glacé icing (see
apricot jam	page 35) or melted
chocolate vermicelli	chocolate

1 Grate the cake into crumbs or rub through a coarse sieve into a mixing bowl.
2 Add the sugar and almonds.
3 Warm the jam over a gentle heat and sieve.
4 Blend the cake and almond mixture to a firm paste with the jam, adding a few drops almonds or rum essence if liked.
5 Shape the mixture into 12–18 balls and leave in a cool place until firm.
6 Dip each ball in glacé icing or melted chocolate, using a skewer.
7 Roll in chocolate vermicelli and leave on a plate until dry.
8 Serve in small paper cases.

Ring doughnuts

cooking time   5–8 minutes

you will need:

6 oz. self-raising flour	1 egg
$\frac{1}{2}$ level teaspoon mixed spice	2$\frac{1}{2}$ tablespoons milk
	2 oz. castor sugar
1 tablespoon blended vegetable oil	pinch salt
	oil for frying

1 Sieve flour, spice and salt into a bowl. Add the sugar.
2 Beat the tablespoon oil, egg and milk together.
3 Stir into the dry ingredients and mix to a soft dough.
4 Turn dough on to a floured surface. Roll out $\frac{1}{4}$-inch thick.
5 Cut into rounds with a 3-inch cutter. Cut out centres, forming rings, with a 1$\frac{1}{2}$-inch cutter.
6 Re-roll remaining pieces of dough. Repeat cutting process.
7 Pour enough oil into a deep frying pan to fill it $\frac{1}{3}$ full.
8 Heat oil to 365°F. (cube of bread will become golden on one side in 30 seconds).
9 Fry doughnuts one at a time until golden, turning them frequently during cooking.
10 Remove from oil with a perforated spoon, leave on crumpled kitchen paper to drain.
11 Toss in castor sugar. Serve on a doily. Makes twelve.

Cinnamon rings

Make as above, omitting mixed spice. Toss rings in castor sugar mixed with powdered cinnamon.

Iced rings

Make as above; when cold, spoon thin white glacé icing (vanilla or lemon flavoured) (see page 35) over the rings. Serve when the icing has set.

Lancashire parkin

cooking time   1–1$\frac{1}{4}$ hours

you will need:

4 oz. flour	4$\frac{1}{2}$ fluid oz. (9 tablespoons) blended vegetable oil
1 level teaspoon baking powder	4 oz. black treacle or syrup
4 oz. fine or medium oatmeal	4 oz. Demerara sugar
3 level teaspoons ground ginger	1 egg
	4 tablespoons milk

1 Grease a shallow 7-inch square tin. Line the bottom with greaseproof paper.

2 Sieve the flour, baking powder, oatmeal and ginger into a large mixing bowl.
3 Heat the oil, treacle or syrup and sugar gently, until the sugar dissolves.
4 Beat the egg and milk together.
5 Make a well in the centre of the dry ingredients, pour in the syrup, then the egg mixture, stirring well until mixture is thoroughly blended.
6 Pour into prepared tin and bake at 335°F.—Mark 3.
7 Leave on a wire tray until cold.
8 Store in a tin for 3–4 days before cutting.

Flapjacks

cooking time   30–35 minutes

you will need:

3 oz. margarine	2 oz. Demerara sugar
4 oz. golden syrup	8 oz. rolled oats

1 Melt the margarine, sugar and syrup together in a saucepan.
2 Add the rolled oats, and mix together thoroughly.
3 Turn the mixture into a greased tin 11$\frac{1}{2}$ × 7$\frac{1}{2}$ inches. Spread over the tin evenly and press down firmly.
4 Bake on the middle shelf of a moderate oven 350°F.—Mark 4.
5 Remove from the oven, cut into sixteen pieces and leave to cool in the tin.

Almond flapjacks

cooking time   20 minutes

you will need:

2 level tablespoons sugar	4 oz. quick porridge oats
2 oz. margarine	1 tablespoon ground almonds
1 tablespoon golden syrup	
$\frac{1}{2}$ teaspoon almond essence	

1 Grease a 6-inch sandwich tin.
2 Heat sugar, margarine and syrup in a pan over a gentle heat.
3 When fat has melted and sugar has dissolved, stir in oats, almonds and essence.
4 Turn mixture into prepared tin and press down evenly.
5 Bake at 375°F.—Mark 5, until firm and golden.
6 Cut into eight pieces while warm.
7 Leave to cool and remove pieces separately on to a wire tray. Leave until cold.

Date shorties

cooking time   20–25 minutes

you will need:

6 oz. self-raising flour	1 tablespoon honey
6 oz. fine semolina	½ level teaspoon ground
8 oz. stoned dates	cinnamon
6 oz. butter	8 tablespoons cold water
3 oz. castor sugar	1 tablespoon lemon juice

1 Grease a Swiss roll tin.
2 Sieve flour and semolina.
3 Melt butter over a gentle heat and add sugar.
4 When sugar is dissolved, stir in flour and semolina.
5 Mix well, spread half this mixture in the tin, press down well.
6 Mix chopped dates, honey, spice, water and lemon juice in a pan. Heat, stirring until soft and smooth.
7 Spread this over crumble in tin. Spread remaining crumble over the top. Press down lightly.
8 Bake in a moderately hot oven 375°F.—Mark 5.
9 Cut into squares at once, but leave in tin until cold. Remove carefully with a palette knife.

Apricot shorties

Make as above, using this apricot filling in place of date mixture.

4 oz. dried apricots	¼ pint water
3 tablespoons sugar	juice ½ lemon

1 Cut apricots roughly with kitchen scissors. Soak for 30 minutes in hot water. Drain.
2 Place apricots, sugar, water and lemon juice in a pan.
3 Cover and simmer until apricots are soft— about 20 minutes.

Quick coconut cones

cooking time   25 minutes

you will need:

6 oz. desiccated coconut	rice paper
about ¼ pint sweetened	2–3 glacé cherries
condensed milk	

1 Put coconut into a bowl and stir in sufficient milk to bind.
2 Cut rice paper into 10–12 squares, place on a lightly greased baking tin.
3 Pile mixture in pyramids, placing one on each square of rice paper. Place a small piece of glacé cherry on each, if liked.
4 Bake in a moderate oven 350°F.—Mark 4, on the middle shelf.
If rice paper is not available, the cones may be cooked on a well greased tin, but care must be taken when removing them. Slide a palette knife under each and lift on to a wire tray.

Quick chocolate cones

Make as before, omitting cherry. When cones are cold, top each with a little melted chocolate, allowing it to run down the cones.

Meringues

cooking time   3–4 hours

you will need:

3 egg whites	3 oz. granulated sugar
pinch salt	3 oz. castor sugar

1 Turn two baking trays upside down and cover with greaseproof paper brushed lightly with oil.
2 Place egg whites in a deep bowl, add the salt.
3 Whisk with a wire whisk or a rotary beater until stiff and 'dry'.
4 Lightly fold in the granulated sugar and continue whisking until mixture regains its former stiffness.
5 Fold in castor sugar (do not disturb mixture more than necessary).
6 Spoon mixture into a large forcing bag fitted with a plain nozzle, and pipe in rounds or cones on to the prepared tins.
7 Dredge with castor sugar and bake in a very slow oven until firm and crisp. Do not allow to brown.
8 Remove tray from oven. Slide each meringue off the tray by slipping a knife underneath. Place on a wire tray until cold (when cold, meringues can be stored several weeks in a tin).
9 Sandwich meringues together with whipped cream or butter cream (see page 33) just before serving.

Note:

Have egg whites as fresh as possible and keep in a cold place until ready to make meringues. If a forcing bag is not available, have 2 dessertspoons in a jug of cold water handy for shaping the meringues. Take up a good spoonful of the mixture in one spoon, smooth it into shape with the second spoon, and lay it on the prepared tin.

Meringues à la Chantilly

Make the meringues as above. Sandwich together with double cream, whisked until thick and flavoured with vanilla essence. A little castor sugar may be added to the cream, if liked.

Meringues marrons glacés

Make meringues as above and sandwich together with chestnut purée and cream.

Cherry meringues

Make meringues as above. Whisk cream until thick and fold in chopped glacé cherries. Flavour with a little cherry brandy, if available.

Chocolate meringues

Make as for plain meringues, adding 1 tablespoon cocoa to the castor sugar. Fold sugar in, in the usual way, but save about 1 level tablespoon. Sprinkle this over the shaped meringues before they are cooked.

Coloured meringues

Tint the mixture pink, green or yellow by adding 1 or 2 drops of colouring after the granulated sugar has been added.

Almond meringue fingers

Make the meringues as above, adding a few drops almond essence to the egg whites. Pipe the meringues in finger lengths on a tin prepared as above. Sprinkle with toasted almonds, roughly chopped, and bake in a slow oven until firm and crisp. When cold, sandwich with butter cream (see page 33).

Fruit-filled meringues

Make meringues as for plain meringues. Pipe mixture in rings, piping two or three rings, one on top of the other to form 'nests'. Bake as for plain meringues. When meringues are required, fill with fresh or drained canned fruit and decorate with whipped cream.

Coffee walnut meringues

Make meringues as for fruit-filled meringues. Fill 'nests' with whipped cream or butter cream flavoured with coffee essence (see page 33) and mixed with chopped walnuts. Decorate the centre of each with a halved walnut.

No-bake fruit cake

you will need:

1 small can evaporated milk	2 oz. glacé cherries, quartered
6 oz. marshmallows	
6 tablespoons orange juice	1 lb. digestive biscuits, crumbed
2 oz. dates, chopped	
6 oz. seedless raisins	1 teaspoon cinnamon
3 oz. chopped walnuts	1 teaspoon nutmeg
4 oz. mixed candied peel, chopped	½ teaspoon mixed spice

1 Line a 2-lb. loaf tin with buttered greaseproof paper.
2 Place marshmallows, milk and orange juice in a pan over a gentle heat. Stir until marshmallows dissolve.
3 Mix together fruit, nuts, crumbs and spice in a large basin.
4 Pour in marshmallow mixture, stir until well blended.
5 Press mixture into tin. Cover lightly with foil, place a weight on top and leave in a refrigerator for at least 24 hours.
6 Turn out and cut into slices.

Chocolate refrigerator cake

you will need:

3 oz. butter	8 oz. digestive (sweetmeal) biscuits
1 oz. sugar	
1 tablespoon syrup	glacé icing (see page 34)
4 oz. plain chocolate	grated chocolate (optional)

1 Brush the inside of a 7-inch flan ring with a little melted butter. Place on a flat plate.
2 Crush biscuits into crumbs, using a rolling pin.
3 Melt the chocolate.
4 Cream the butter and sugar. Beat in the syrup and chocolate.
5 Add the crumbs, and pack the mixture into flan ring. Smooth the top.
6 Place in the refrigerator for at least 3 hours.
7 Remove the flan ring. Spread the top with glacé icing (see page 35), flavoured with lemon or orange juice. Decorate with coarsely grated chocolate if liked.

Orange cream pie

you will need:

6 oz. digestive (sweetmeal) biscuits	1 small can evaporated milk
3 oz. butter, melted	2 teaspoons lemon juice
½ orange jelly	grated chocolate (optional)
1 can mandarin oranges	

1 Put the biscuits between two sheets of greaseproof paper or foil.
2 Roll with a rolling pin until the biscuits are crushed into fine crumbs.
3 Put the crumbs into a bowl, stir in the butter and mix well.

4 Brush an 8-inch pie plate with melted butter. Press the crumb mixture over the bottom and sides of the plate. Leave in a cold place to set.

5 Drain the juice from the mandarin oranges. Measure ¼ pint of the juice and bring to the boil in a small pan.

6 Pour the juice on to the jelly and stir until the jelly is dissolved. Leave in a cool place until thick.

7 Meanwhile, pour the milk into a basin, add the lemon juice and whisk until thick.

8 Whisk the milk into the jelly and continue whisking until the mixture is thick and fluffy.

9 Chop half the mandarin oranges, stir into the jelly mixture and pile into the prepared case.

10 Leave to set. Decorate with remaining mandarin oranges and sprinkle with grated chocolate.

4 To make the filling, place the water, gelatine, lemon rind and sugar in a saucepan.

5 Heat gently until almost boiling, stirring all the time.

6 Remove from the heat, add the lemon juice and leave until cold, but not set.

7 Whisk egg whites until stiff, and whisk in the cooled liquid. Continue whisking until mixture is thick and nearly set.

8 Pile the mixture into the prepared case.

9 Halve the remaining gingersnaps and arrange around the edge of the plate, pressing the cut side of the biscuits into the mixture.

10 Decorate with diamonds of angelica.

Lemon cream pie

you will need:

6 oz. digestive (sweetmeal) bisuits
3 oz. butter, melted
1 lemon jelly
1 small can evaporated milk
grated rind and juice ½ lemon
milk chocolate flake

1 Prepare the biscuit crust as for orange cream pie.

2 Dissolve the jelly in a little boiling water and make up to ½ pint with cold water. Leave in a cool place until thick and just about to set.

3 Whisk the milk with the lemon juice and rind until thick.

4 Whisk the milk into the jelly and pour into the prepared case.

5 Leave in a cold place to set. When set, decorate with crumbled chocolate flake.

Lemon frosted pie

you will need:

1 lb. gingersnap biscuits
3 oz. butter
2 oz. sugar
½ teaspoon cinnamon

filling:
½ pint cold water
½ oz. gelatine
rind and juice 2 lemons
2 egg whites
angelica

1 Crush half the biscuits with a rolling pin.

2 Place in a bowl. Melt the butter and stir into the crumbs, adding the sugar and spice.

3 Mix well and press round the sides and bottom of a buttered 8-inch ovenproof plate. Leave in a cold place until set (or bake in a moderately hot oven for 10 minutes, then leave until cold).

Oranges and lemons pie

Made as for lemon frosted pie, using a small can mandarin oranges. Drain the oranges and make the juice up to ½ pint with water. Use this liquid for dissolving the gelatine. Decorate with mandarin oranges.

Fruity halva

you will need:

4 oz. butter
4 oz. fine semolina
2 oz. raisins, seeded and chopped
1 oz. glacé cherries, chopped
1 oz. candied mixed peel, finely chopped
2 oz. fine coconut
½ teaspoon vanilla or almond essence
6 oz. sugar
¼ pint water

1 Melt the butter, stir in the semolina and brown slightly.

2 Add the raisins, cherries, peel, coconut and essence.

3 Boil the sugar and water until thick and syrupy, removing it from the heat before it changes colour.

4 Stir in the semolina mixture and cook over a low heat, stirring until thick.

5 Pour into an oiled shallow dish and mark into squares.

6 Allow to set, and when firm, cut into squares. Serve with coffee.

Pastries

Pastry can be used in dozens of ways to make delicious tea-time treats, and it forms the basis of many popular cakes. In this section, you will find recipes for making pastry and plenty of ideas for using it.

Shortcrust pastry

you will need:

8 oz. flour
pinch salt
2 oz. margarine

2 oz. lard (or vegetable shortening)
cold water to mix

1 Sieve the flour and salt into a mixing bowl.
2 Chop the fat roughly and add to the flour. Rub the fat into the flour, using the fingertips, until the mixture resembles breadcrumbs.
3 Add cold water gradually and knead mixture lightly by hand until it works together into a firm dough.
4 Turn out on to a lightly floured surface and knead lightly until smooth. Turn pastry over and roll out as required.

Rich shortcrust pastry or flan pastry

you will need:

8 oz. flour
pinch salt
5 oz. butter

1 teaspoon castor sugar
1 egg yolk
1–2 tablespoons cold water

1 Sieve the flour and salt into a bowl.
2 Rub the butter lightly into the flour, using the fingertips, until the mixture resembles breadcrumbs.
3 Add sugar and egg yolk, work into the flour, adding water gradually until mixture forms a firm dough.
4 Turn on to a floured surface, knead lightly and roll out. If the pastry is difficult to handle, leave in a cold place for at least half an hour before using.

To make a flan case

1 Make pastry as above.
2 Roll out pastry into a circle about 2 inches larger than the flan ring.
3 Place flan ring on a baking sheet. Place the round of pastry over the ring and press into shape, taking care that the pastry fits well against the inside edge, but that it is not stretched.
4 Trim off surplus pastry, by passing the rolling pin over the edge of the ring. Place a piece of lightly greased greaseproof paper, greased side down, in the flan and fill the flan with uncooked rice, haricot beans or macaroni.
5 Bake in a hot oven 400°F.—Mark 6, until the pastry is firm—15 minutes. Pastry baked in this way is described as 'baked blind'. This is done to ensure a good shape. The rice, etc., can be stored in a jar and used indefinitely for this purpose.
6 Remove filling and paper from flan. Return flan to oven for a further 15 minutes to allow base to cook through.
7 Remove flan ring and leave flan case on a wire tray until cold. Cold cooked pastry cases may be stored in an air-tight tin and used as required.
If a flan ring is not available, a sandwich tin may be used, but strips of strong paper should be placed across the inside of the tin to protrude at the edge, before the pastry is fitted. This will enable the flan case to be removed easily from the tin after cooking.

Fork-mix pastry

you will need:

8 oz. flour
½ teaspoon salt

2 tablespoons cold water
4 oz. instant creaming vegetable fat

1 Sieve the flour and salt into a bowl.
2 Add the water, and fat in one piece.
3 Use a large fork and mix to a dough.
This is a quick method for making shortcrust pastry.

Jellied fruit flan

Fill a cooked flan case with drained, canned fruit. Heat $\frac{1}{4}$ pint fruit juice in a small pan, stir in 2 teaspoons powdered gelatine. Heat gently until the gelatine dissolves; add sugar to taste. Leave in a cool place until just about to set. Spoon over the fruit, and leave until completely set.

Tartlets

Make 6 oz. shortcrust pastry. Roll out thinly and cut into rounds with a fluted cutter (a little larger than the patty tins being used). Line 12–15 patty tins with the pastry, pressing it well in with the fingers.

Jam tartlets

Half fill each with jam and bake in a hot oven 400°F.—Mark 6 for 15–20 minutes.

Syrup tartlets

Half fill with a mixture of 2 large tablespoons warmed syrup, 2 tablespoons cake or breadcrumbs and the juice of $\frac{1}{2}$ lemon.

Alternatively, the tartlets may be prepared and baked as above and filled with any of the following fillings.

1 Cream 3 oz. butter with 3 oz. sugar. Beat in 2 eggs. Stir in 1 oz. cornflour, blended with 2 tablespoons milk, 1 oz. ground almonds, 2 oz. cake crumbs, 1 teaspoon cinnamon and 1 dessertspoon lemon juice.
2 Cream 4 oz. butter with 4 oz. sugar. Add the grated rind of 1 lemon. Beat in 2 eggs and the juice of the lemon. Leave in a cool place for 24 hours before baking.
3 Cream 2 oz. butter with 2 oz. sugar. Beat in 2 egg yolks. Add 2 oz. ground almonds, 1 level tablespoon cornflour and a few drops vanilla essence. Fold in the stiffly whisked egg whites. Put a small spoonful of jam in each patty case and fill with the mixture.
4 Cream 3 oz. butter with 3 oz. sugar. Add the finely grated rind of 2 oranges. Beat in 2 egg yolks. Blend 1 teaspoon cornflour with the juice of 1 orange. Add to the creamed mixture, with 1$\frac{1}{2}$ oz. cake crumbs. Fold in the stiffly whisked egg whites. Coat finished tartlets with glacé icing (see page 34), if liked.

Pineapple cream tarts

cooking time   10–12 minutes

you will need:

4 oz. shortcrust pastry	1 16-oz. can pineapple
2 oz. butter	pieces
6 oz. icing sugar	1 tablespoon pineapple
glacé cherries	syrup, boiling

1 Line twelve patty tins with the pastry.
2 Bake blind in a hot oven and leave to cool.
3 Cream butter and sugar, adding the syrup,
4 Fold in $\frac{3}{4}$ pineapple pieces, drained and chopped.
5 Pile into the pastry cases, top with remaining pineapple and decorate each with a cherry.

Strawberry tartlets

Line 12 fluted tartlet tins with pastry and bake as above. When cold, fill with ripe, fresh strawberries. Melt 2 tablespoons redcurrant jelly (or strained strawberry or raspberry jam) in a saucepan with 1 tablespoon water. Mix well, and brush over the fruit to give a glaze.

Surprise tartlets

Prepare tartlet cases as above. When cold, put a little apricot jam in the bottom of each. Make small balls of almond paste (see page 37). Dip these on the end of a skewer into thin glacé icing (see page 34). Use different coloured icing if available—some of the balls may be dipped in melted chocolate. Leave on a plate until set. Place two or three balls into each pastry case. Maraschino or glacé cherries, or a pineapple cube, may be added, too, if liked.

Macaroon pastries

cooking time   30 minutes

you will need:

4 oz. rich shortcrust pastry	1 oz. flour
jam	5 oz. castor sugar
4 oz. ground almonds	2 egg whites

1 Line patty or boat-shaped tins with pastry, put a little jam in the bottom of each.
2 Mix almonds, flour and sugar. Whisk egg whites until stiff.
3 Fold the dry ingredients into the egg whites. Spoon the mixture into the pastry cases. Cut small strips of remaining pastry and arrange two strips across each tart.
4 Bake in a hot oven 400°F.—Mark 6.
The crosses of pastry may be omitted and a halved blanched almond or glacé cherry pressed into the centre of each.

Chocolate almond pastries

Make as above, omitting pastry crosses. Allow tarts to cool and coat with chocolate glacé icing (see page 35).

Cherry macaroon pastries

Make as above, putting a little chopped glacé or maraschino cherry in the bottom of each tart instead of jam. Coat the finished tarts with lemon flavoured glacé icing (see page 35).

Macaroon drops

Cut pastry into rounds with a 2-inch fluted cutter. Place on a baking sheet. Heap a little almond mixture on to each. Bake for about 20 minutes. Coat with icing when cold. Sprinkle with chopped toasted almonds or grated chocolate.

Pineapple and mincemeat slices

Line a shallow oblong tin with shortcrust pastry. Crimp edges and prick with a fork. Spread with mincemeat and cover with drained crushed pineapple. Cover with another piece of pastry and seal the edges. Brush with beaten egg and sprinkle with sugar. Bake at 425°F.—Mark 7. When cold, cut into slices.

Jam and coconut slices

Make as above, spreading the pastry with raspberry jam mixed with an equal quantity of coconut.

Apricot almond slices

Make as above, spreading pastry with apricot jam and sprinkling it with ground almonds.

Raisin cakes

cooking time   15–20 minutes

you will need:

4 oz. shortcrust pastry	about 2 tablespoons lemon
8 oz. seedless raisins	juice
6 walnut halves	1 oz. brown sugar

1 Line 10 patty tins with the pastry.
2 Mince the raisins and nuts, or chop very finely.
3 Moisten with lemon juice, add half the sugar.
4 Put a spoonful of the mixture into each pastry case and sprinkle with sugar.
5 Bake in a hot oven 400°F.—Mark 6.

Canadian cakes

cooking time   15–20 minutes

you will need:

6 oz. shortcrust pastry	4 oz. sugar
1 egg	½ oz. melted butter
4 oz. currants	⅛ pint double cream (optional)

1 Line 15 patty tins with the pastry.
2 Beat the egg, adding the currants, sugar and melted butter. Mix well.
3 Place a little mixture in each patty case.
4 Bake in a hot oven 400°F.—Mark 6.
5 Leave on a wire tray to cool.
6 Top each with a spoonful of whipped cream, if liked.

Bakewell tart

cooking time   30–40 minutes

you will need:

4 oz. shortcrust pastry	1 egg
raspberry jam	2 oz. ground almonds
2 oz. butter	1–2 drops almond essence
2 oz. sugar	icing sugar

1 Line a flan tin or sandwich tin with shortcrust pastry, spread with jam.
2 Cream butter and sugar, gradually beat in the egg and add the essence.
3 Stir in the almonds and spread the mixture over the jam.
4 Bake in a hot oven 400°F.—Mark 6, until the filling is set and golden.
5 Dredge with icing sugar.

Custard tart

cooking time   about 1 hour

you will need:

6 oz. shortcrust pastry	vanilla essence
2 eggs	1 small can evaporated
1 oz. castor sugar	milk
	grated nutmeg

1 Line a deep pie plate with pastry, pressing the pastry well against the bottom and sides of the plate.
2 Beat the eggs and sugar together in a basin, adding the vanilla essence.
3 Pour the evaporated milk into a measuring jug and make up to ¼ pint with water.
4 Heat the milk in a pan, pour on to the egg mixture, stirring carefully.
5 Pour the custard into the pastry case and sprinkle with grated nutmeg.
6 Bake in a slow oven 335°F.—Mark 3, until the custard is set.

Apricot custard tart

Make as before, covering the base of the tart with dried apricots which have been soaked overnight and stewed in a little water.

Mincemeat custard tart

Make as before, spreading pastry with mincemeat before filling with custard.

Coconut custard tart

Make as before, spreading pastry with raspberry jam. Omit the nutmeg and sprinkle finished tart with toasted coconut.

Custard tartlets

Make as before, lining deep patty tins with pastry. Fill with custard and bake for about 20 minutes.

Lemon meringue pie

cooking time   10–15 minutes

you will need:

7-inch baked flan case	nut of butter
filling:	**meringue:**
1 oz. cornflour	1 egg white
3–4 oz. sugar	pinch salt
1 egg yolk	1 oz. sugar
½ pint water	1 level teaspoon
1 large lemon	cornflour

1 Make the filling. Mix the cornflour, sugar and egg yolk smoothly with a little of the cold water.
2 Put the rest of the water on to heat with the thinly peeled lemon rind.
3 Strain on to the cornflour mixture, return to the pan and cook for 3 minutes, stirring throughout.
4 Remove from the heat, stir in the butter and the lemon juice. Turn into the baked pastry case.
5 Make the meringue. Beat the egg white until stiff with the pinch of salt.
6 Mix the sugar and cornflour together, and fold lightly into the beaten egg white.
7 Pile on top of the pie.
8 Place in a moderate oven 350°F.—Mark 4, for 10–15 minutes, until golden.

Frangipane tart

cooking time   25–30 minutes

you will need:

4 oz. rich shortcrust pastry (see page 52)	1 teaspoon flour
2 oz. sugar	2 oz. ground almonds
2 oz. butter	icing sugar or lemon flavoured glacé icing
1 egg	(see page 35)

1 Line a 7-inch pie plate with the pastry.
2 Cream the fat and sugar, and beat in the egg.
3 Stir in the flour and ground almonds.
4 Spread the almond mixture into the pastry case.
5 Bake in a moderate oven 350°F.—Mark 4.
6 Leave until cold, then dust with icing sugar or spread with the glacé icing.

Canadian apple tart

cooking time   30–40 minutes

you will need:

6 oz. shortcrust pastry	4 oz. brown sugar
1 lb. cooking apples	1 oz. butter

1 Line an 8-inch pie plate with pastry and prick well with a fork.
2 Peel and core the apples, cut into slices and arrange over the pastry.
3 Sprinkle thickly with sugar and dot with butter.
4 Bake in a hot oven 425°F.—Mark 7, for 10 minutes, then reduce heat to 400°F.—Mark 6, and cook until golden. Serve hot or cold.

Florentine tart

Prepare as above, baking the pastry 'blind'. Stew the apples with sugar and grated nutmeg to taste. Allow the apples to cool, spread over pastry and top with meringue (made from 2 egg whites and 4 oz. sugar). Bake in a cool oven until meringue is firm.

Date tart

cooking time   30 minutes

you will need:

6 oz. shortcrust pastry	3 egg whites
4 oz. dates	2 oz. ground almonds
rum or brandy	4 oz. castor sugar

1 Line an 8-inch pie plate with the pastry, and prick lightly with a fork.
2 Chop the dates and soak in the rum for 20 minutes.
3 Whisk the egg whites until stiff and fold in the sugar.
4 Stir in the almonds and dates.
5 Pile into the pastry case and bake at 425°F.—Mark 7.
6 Sprinkle with castor sugar and leave until cold.

Apple date tart

Make as above, spreading the pastry with sweetened stewed apples before piling on the meringue mixture.

Queens tart

cooking time   40 minutes

you will need:

6 oz. shortcrust pastry or flan pastry	3 oz. flour
	a little milk
3 oz. margarine	2–3 oz. glacé cherries
3 oz. sugar	glacé icing (see page 34)
1 egg	

1 Line an 8-inch pie plate with pastry and prick lightly with a fork.
2 Cream margarine and sugar, and gradually beat in the egg.
3 Fold in the flour, adding enough milk to make a soft consistency.
4 Stir in the cherries and spread mixture into the pastry case.
5 Bake at 425°F.—Mark 7. Leave until cold, then spread with white glacé icing flavoured with almond essence or lemon juice. Decorate with halved glacé cherries.

Princess tart

Make as above, adding chopped mixed peel instead of cherries and ice with lemon glacé icing (see page 35).

Yorkshire cheese cake

cooking time   30–40 minutes

you will need:

1 pint milk	4 oz. sugar
rennet	1 oz. currants
6 oz. shortcrust pastry	1 oz. candied peel
2 small eggs	2 teaspoons baking powder
2 oz. butter	a little grated nutmeg
¼ teaspoon salt	

1 Prepare junket with the milk, following the instructions on the rennet bottle. When the junket is set, cut it up, tie in muslin and allow to drip. When well drained, beat up the curds with a fork.
2 Make shortcrust pastry and use to line a deep pie plate; decorate the edges.
3 Beat the eggs, melt the butter and beat into the curds with all the other ingredients, adding the baking powder last.
4 Fill the pastry case and sprinkle with a little nutmeg.
5 Bake in a hot oven 400°F.—Mark 6, until pastry is cooked and the filling lightly set.

Apple dumplings

cooking time   30 minutes

you will need:

8 oz. shortcrust pastry	2 oz. brown sugar
4 medium-sized cooking apples	ground cinnamon
	8 cloves (optional)

1 Divide the pastry into four and roll each piece into a round.
2 Peel and core the apples, and place one on each round of pastry.
3 Moisten the pastry, work it round the apple until it is almost covered.
4 Fill the core cavity of each with brown sugar, mixed with cinnamon to taste and 2 cloves, if liked.
5 Bring the pastry together so that the apple is completely covered, pressing the edges of pastry firmly to seal.
6 Place the apples, join side down, on a greased baking tray. Brush each with milk and sprinkle with sugar.
7 Bake in a hot oven 400°F.—Mark 6, until golden.
8 Serve hot or cold.

The apples may be filled with brown sugar blended with an equal quantity of butter and flavoured with lemon rind, finely grated, or with honey mixed with ground almonds or with mincemeat. They may also be filled with mixed dried fruit and butter, chopped dates or stewed dried apricots.

Pear dumplings

Prepare the pastry as for apple dumplings. Choose firm small pears. Peel them, cut in half and remove the core. Put a knob of spiced butter (see page 61) in the core cavity of one half of each pear. Put the pear halves together again, cover with pastry and finish as above, allowing 35–40 minutes cooking time.

Flaky pastry

you will need:

8 oz. flour	squeeze lemon juice
pinch salt	cold water to mix
6 oz. fat—use butter or equal quantities margarine and lard	

1 Sieve flour and salt into a bowl.
2 Cream the fat until soft and pliable, and divide into four portions.
3 Rub one portion of the fat into the flour, add a squeeze of lemon juice and sufficient cold water to make a soft dough.

4 Roll the dough into an oblong. Cover $\frac{2}{3}$ of this with another portion of the fat, dabbing the fat in small pieces over the dough.

5 Fold the dough in three, starting at the bottom with the uncovered section. Bring this up to the centre of the oblong. Bring the top third down over this. Lightly press the edges together with a rolling pin.

6 Half turn the pastry to the left and roll it out into an oblong.

7 Repeat this process (Nos. 5 and 6) twice, adding another portion of the fat each time.

8 Fold the pastry in three once more, without adding fat.
Wrap the pastry in greaseproof paper or foil, and leave in the 'fridge or a cold place for an hour before rolling out for use.
If possible leave the pastry to 'relax' in a cool place for about 10 minutes between each rolling.

Puff pastry

you will need:

8 oz. flour
pinch salt
squeeze lemon juice

8 oz. unsalted butter
cold water to mix

1 Sieve the flour and salt, and rub in 1 oz. of the butter.

2 Add the lemon juice and sufficient water to mix to a soft dough.

3 Turn dough on to a floured surface and knead lightly until smooth. Roll out into a square.

4 Form the butter into an oblong. Place it on the bottom half of the pastry. Fold the top half of the pastry over the butter and seal the edges with a rolling pin.

5 Turn the pastry so that the fold is to the right. Roll it out into a strip, fold it into three and seal the edges.

6 Half turn the pastry and repeat the rolling and folding (No. 5) six times in all.
If possible make this pastry the day before it is required, to allow it to become firm and cold before it is finally rolled out and cut.

Rough puff pastry

you will need:

8 oz. flour
pinch salt
6 oz. butter—or equal
  quantities of margarine
  and lard

1 teaspoon lemon juice
cold water to mix

1 Sieve flour and salt into a bowl.

2 Cut the fat into small cubes, add to the flour. Do not rub in.

3 Add lemon juice and sufficient cold water to mix to a fairly stiff dough.

4 Roll out into an oblong, taking care not to stretch the pastry at the edges.

5 Fold the pastry into three. Bring the bottom end two thirds across, and bring the top piece down to the folded edge.

6 Seal the edges by pressing lightly with a rolling pin.

7 Half turn the pastry to the left and roll it out into an oblong.

8 Repeat this process (Nos. 5 and 6) twice.

9 Fold the pastry in three once more, wrap it in greaseproof paper or foil and leave it in a 'fridge or cold place for an hour before rolling out for use.
This pastry is very similar to puff pastry but is easier and quicker to make. It can be used in any recipe which requires puff or flaky pastry.

Petites mille feuilles

cooking time   8 minutes

you will need:

6 oz. puff or rough puff
  pastry
1 egg
  apricot jam

$\frac{1}{4}$ pint double cream
almonds, blanched and
  chopped

1 Roll out pastry $\frac{1}{8}$-inch thick.

2 Cut in small rounds, using a 2-inch cutter. Place on a baking sheet.

3 Brush with beaten egg and prick with a fork.

4 Bake in a very hot oven 470°F.—Mark 9, until golden brown.

5 Cool on a wire tray. Sandwich three rounds of pastry with apricot jam and cream, whipped until thick.

6 Brush top lightly with jam and sprinkle with nuts.

Petites lemon mille feuilles

Make as above. Sandwich layers of pastry with lemon curd and cream. Spoon a little lemon flavoured glacé icing (see page 35) on the top of each and sprinkle with nuts.

Raspberry mille feuilles

Cut four rounds of puff or rough puff pastry about 8 inches in diameter. Bake in a very hot oven for about 10 minutes. When cold, sandwich with crushed raspberries, sprinkled with castor sugar and whipped cream. Cover top with glacé icing (see page 34) and decorate with whole raspberries or almonds.

Cream horns

Roll flaky or puff pastry thinly into an oblong 12 inches long. Cut into 1-inch strips. Moisten edge of each strip and roll round a cream horn tin. Start at the pointed end of the tin and overlap the pastry slightly. Bake in a very hot oven 470°F.—Mark 9, until crisp—10–15 minutes. Slip off tins and leave until cold. Place a good spoonful of jam in each, fill up with whipped cream and dredge with icing sugar.

Almond pastries

Line boat-shaped or patty tins with rough puff or puff pastry. Half fill with soft almond paste (see page 37). Cover with a pastry top, seal and flute the edges. Brush with beaten egg, make 2–3 small cuts in the top of each and bake at 425°F.—Mark 7, for 20–30 minutes. Dredge with icing sugar and serve hot or cold.

Danish almond pastries

Make as above, placing a little chopped mixed peel in each pastry case before adding the almond paste. When pastries are cold, coat top with lemon flavoured glacé icing (see page 35).

Nut and spice twists

A good way to use up scraps of pastry.
Roll out puff or flaky pastry thinly and cut into strips, 1½ inches wide and 3 inches long. Brush with egg white and sprinkle with chopped almonds and a pinch of mixed spice or cinnamon. Twist each strip at both ends. Bake in a very hot oven until golden brown— 5–8 minutes. Dredge with icing sugar.

Jam puffs

Roll out rough puff or puff pastry ⅛-inch thick and cut into four rounds. Spread jam over half of each. Brush edges of circle with beaten egg, fold over and seal. 'Knock up' with the back of a knife and make small flutes around the edge. Brush with beaten egg, sprinkle with castor sugar, and make one or two slits in the top of each. Bake in a very hot oven for about 10 minutes until golden brown.

Apple puffs

Make as above, using sweetened apple purée instead of jam. Sprinkle puffs with castor sugar mixed with a little cinnamon.

Cream slices

cooking time   10–15 minutes

you will need:

6 oz. puff pastry
raspberry or strawberry
  jam

whipped cream or
  confectioner's custard
  (see page 61)
white glacé icing (see
  page 34)

1 Roll out the pastry, ¼-inch thick, into a strip 4 inches wide.
2 Cut into 1½ inch pieces and place on a baking sheet. Bake in a very hot oven 470°F.—Mark 9, until well risen and golden. Leave to cool on a wire tray.
3 When cold, sandwich two slices together with jam and cream or custard.
4 Coat the top of each slice with glacé icing.

French cream slices

Make as above. Sprinkle glacé icing with slivers of toasted almonds. When icing sets, dredge each slice with dry icing sugar.

Lemon hearts

Roll puff pastry out into a piece ¼-inch thick. Cut out with a heart shaped cutter. Bake in a very hot oven for 10 minutes. When cold, cut through with a sharp knife and sandwich together with lemon curd. Coat top with lemon glacé icing (see page 35) and decorate with small pieces of angelica and halved glacé cherries.

Devonshire hearts

Make as for lemon hearts. Sandwich pastry with strawberry jam and whipped cream. Dredge with icing sugar before serving.

Eccles cakes

cooking time   15–20 minutes

you will need:

6 oz. flaky pastry
egg white to glaze
castor sugar
filling:
1 oz. butter

4 oz. currants
1–2 oz. chopped peel
good pinch grated nutmeg
good pinch mixed spice
1 oz. sugar

1 Make the filling by melting the butter and adding the fruit, sugar and spice.
2 Roll out the pastry, ¼ inch thick, and cut into rounds with a large cutter.
3 Place a spoonful of filling on each round, damp the edges of the pastry and draw them together to enclose the filling.

4 Turn cakes over so that the smooth side is uppermost, flatten slightly with the rolling pin. Make three cuts across the top of each.

5 Place on a baking tray, brush with egg white and dredge with castor sugar.

6 Bake at 425°F.—Mark 7, until golden. Cool on a wire tray.

Banbury cakes

cooking time   20 minutes

you will need:

8 oz. flaky pastry	2 oz. sugar
egg white and sugar to glaze	grated nutmeg
filling:	mixed spice
2 oz. currants	lemon juice
2 oz. raisins	1 dessertspoon brandy
2 oz. chopped peel	2 teaspoons cake crumbs

Make as for eccles cake (page 58), cutting pastry into rounds 3–4 inches in diameter. Form into ovals, cut a cross on the top of each, allowing the filling to show through. Brush with egg white, sprinkle with castor sugar and bake.

Cumberland slices

Line a shallow oblong tin with pastry. Sprinkle with mixed dried fruit and dot with butter. Cover with second piece of pastry. Damp and seal the edges. Bake in a hot oven 425°F.—Mark 7, for 30 minutes. Brush with egg white, dredge with castor sugar and bake for a further 5 minutes. Cut into slices and serve hot or cold.

Mincemeat slices

Make as above, spreading pastry with mincemeat instead of fruit and omitting the butter. The mincemeat may be mixed with marmalade or stewed apple, if liked.

Maids of honour

cooking time   25–30 minutes

you will need:

4 oz. puff pastry	½ oz. flour
4 oz. ground almonds	2 tablespoons cream
2 oz. castor sugar	1 tablespoon orange flower water (obtainable from chemists)
1 egg	

1 Roll out the pastry thinly and line twelve patty tins.

2 Mix the ground almonds and castor sugar together.

3 Beat in the egg, flour, cream and orange flower water.

4 Put a little of the mixture into each patty case.

5 Bake in a hot oven 400°F.—Mark 6, until set and golden brown.

6 Cool on a wire tray.

Apple puffs

cooking time   15–20 minutes

you will need:

8 oz. flaky pastry	pinch powdered cloves or cinnamon
2–3 cooking apples	egg white and sugar to glaze
brown sugar	

1 Roll pastry into an oblong ⅛-inch thick. Cut into six squares and brush with water.

2 Peel, core and slice the apples.

3 Place some apple slices on each square of pastry. Sprinkle with sugar and a pinch of spice.

4 Damp the edges of pastry, fold over to form a triangle.

5 Press the edges firmly together and flute the edges.

6 Place on a greased baking sheet. Brush with egg white and sprinkle with sugar.

7 Bake in a very hot oven 450°F.—Mark 8.

Almond puff

cooking time   about 30 minutes

you will need:

6 oz. puff or rough puff pastry	1 oz. butter
1½ oz. ground almonds	1 teaspoon flour
1 egg	1 tablespoon rum
	icing sugar

1 Divide pastry in half, roll out into two rounds, 7–8 inches in diameter.

2 Brush a baking sheet with cold water. Place one round of pastry on this.

3 Separate the egg. Mix yolk with the almonds and butter. Add flour and sufficient rum to make a soft paste.

4 Spread the paste over the round of pastry on the tin. Damp edges of the pastry and cover with second round. Seal edges and flute.

5 Brush top with egg white, score with a sharp knife.

6 Bake in a very hot oven 450°F.—Mark 8, for about 30 minutes.

7 Remove from the oven when cooked, dredge with icing sugar.

8 Return to the oven for 2–3 minutes longer. Cool on a wire tray. Sprinkle with more sugar, if liked.

Lemon almond puff

Make as above, adding the finely grated rind of ½ lemon to the almonds, and flavour with lemon juice in place of the rum.

Mincemeat almond puff

Make as above, omit the filling. Spread bottom layer of pastry with mincemeat, sprinkle with ground almonds and finish as almond puff.

Mince pies

1 Roll out flaky, rough puff or shortcrust pastry about ⅛-inch thick.
2 Cut out enough small rounds of pastry to make a lid for each pie.
3 Knead all the scraps of pastry lightly together and roll out.
4 Cut out rounds to line patty tins, making them a size larger than the tin.
5 Line the tins with pastry, fill with mincemeat and damp the edges.
6 Put on the lids, seal and flute the edges. Make a small hole in the centre of each.
7 Brush each pie with egg white and sprinkle with sugar.
8 Bake in a very hot oven 450°F.—Mark 8, for 20–30 minutes, if using flaky or rough puff. Bake at 400°F.—Mark 6, if using shortcrust pastry.

Choux pastry (basic recipe)

you will need:

¼ pint water	2 oz. plain flour
1 oz. butter	1 egg white
pinch salt	2 egg yolks

1 Heat the water and butter, with the salt, in a small pan.
2 Bring to the boil, add the flour and beat well with a wooden spoon.
3 Remove from the heat and continue beating until the mixture is smooth and leaves the sides of the pan.
4 Allow to cool, then beat in the egg gradually.

Chocolate éclairs

cooking time   30–35 minutes

1 Make choux pastry as before.
2 Put mixture into a piping bag with a ½-inch plain nozzle.
3 Pipe in six 3-inch lengths on a greased baking tray.
4 Bake in a hot oven 400°F.—Mark 6.
5 Remove from tray, make a small slit in the side of each to allow the steam to escape.
6 When cool, fill each with sweetened whipped cream or confectioner's custard (see page 61).
7 Coat the top of each with chocolate glacé icing (see page 35).

Cream buns

cooking time   20–30 minutes

1 Make the choux pastry, as before.
2 Put into a piping bag with a ½-inch plain nozzle.
3 Pipe in six small rounds at least 3 inches apart on a greased baking sheet. Cover with an inverted roasting tin.
4 Bake in a hot oven 400°F.—Mark 6.
5 Remove on to a wire tray, making a small slit in the side of each to allow the steam to escape.
6 When cool, fill each with sweetened whipped cream or confectioner's custard (see page 61).
7 Dredge each with icing sugar or coat top with coffee glacé icing (see page 35).

Profiteroles

cooking time   30–35 minutes

1 Make choux pastry.
2 Pipe with a ½-inch plain nozzle in four rounds on a greased baking tray. Cover with an inverted roasting tin.
3 Bake in a hot oven 400°F.—Mark 6.
4 Remove on to a wire tray to cool, making a slit in each to allow steam to escape.
5 Fill each with whipped cream.
6 Serve coated with hot chocolate sauce.

Danish pastry

cooking time   12–15 minutes

you will need:

8 oz. plain flour	1 oz. lard
pinch salt	1 level tablespoon castor
1 egg	sugar
4 tablespoons cold water	½ oz. yeast creamed with
5 oz. Danish butter	1 tablespoon water

1 Sieve flour and salt into a bowl and rub in the lard.

2 Add the egg, sugar and water to the creamed yeast.

3 Pour into the flour mixture and mix to a soft dough.

4 Turn the dough out of the bowl and knead lightly until smooth.

5 Cover and allow to rest in a cool place for 10 minutes.

6 Beat the butter until soft and shape into an oblong block about ½ inch thick.

7 Roll out the dough into a square, slightly larger than the butter.

8 Place the butter in the centre of the dough, fold the sides of the dough over the butter, so that they overlap down the centre. Seal in the butter, by pressing lightly with the rolling pin.

9 Roll dough into an oblong strip about three times as long as it is wide. Fold evenly in three, cover and leave for 10 minutes.

10 Repeat rolling and folding twice more, cover and leave to rest for a further 10 minutes in a cool place. Roll out and use as required.

Butter horns

1 Make dough as above and cut in half.

2 Roll one piece of dough into a circle about 9 inches across. Trim to a good shape, if necessary.

3 Divide circle into eight sections. Cut a small slit lengthways near the pointed end of each section. Place a small piece of almond paste (see below) in the middle of the short side of each.

4 Roll up each section from the short side to the point and curl into a crescent shape.

5 Place on a greased baking sheet, about 1 inch apart. Brush with beaten egg.

6 Leave in a slightly warm place to prove for 15–20 minutes.

7 Bake in a hot oven 425°F.—Mark 7.

8 Brush with glacé icing (see page 34) while still warm, and sprinkle with flaked, blanched almonds.

9 Roll out second piece of dough and finish in the same way. Each piece of dough makes eight horns.

Imperial stars

1 Make Danish pastry dough (page 60) and cut in half.

2 Roll out dough into a rectangle 12 × 6 inches, and cut into eight 3-inch squares.

3 Place a small piece of almond paste (see below) in the centre of each square.

4 Make a diagonal slit from each corner, half way to the centre of each square.

5 Fold the right-hand point of the sections to the centre of each square. Press firmly into position and brush with beaten egg.

6 Place on a greased baking sheet, leave to prove for 15–20 minutes.

7 Bake at 425°F.—Mark 7.

8 Pipe a swirl of confectioner's custard (see below) into the centre of each, or drop a teaspoon of glacé icing (see page 34) into the centre, and stud with half a glacé cherry. Finish other piece of dough in the same way. Each piece of dough makes eight stars.

Fruit whirls

1 Make Danish pastry dough (page 60) and cut in half.

2 Roll one piece of dough into an oblong 12 × 8 inches.

3 Spread dough with spiced butter (see below), and sprinkle with a few sultanas and some finely chopped peel.

4 Cut strip of dough in half lengthways. Roll each piece up from the short end to make a fat roll about 4 inches wide. Cut into four 1-inch slices.

5 Place cut-side down on a greased baking sheet and brush with egg.

6 Prove and bake as for previous recipe.

7 To finish, coat with glacé icing (see page 34) and sprinkle with chopped almonds.

Spiced butter

Cream 2 oz. butter with 2 oz. icing sugar and 2 level teaspoons cinnamon.

Confectioner's custard

Blend 2 egg yolks, 1 oz. castor sugar and ¼ oz. flour to a smooth paste. Stir in ½ pint boiling milk. Return to the heat and stir until just boiling, remove from heat and add a few drops vanilla essence. Leave until cold.

Almond paste for Danish pastries

Blend 2 oz. ground almonds with 2 oz. castor sugar and enough egg white to make a stiff paste. Add 3–4 drops almond essence.

Biscuits and Cookies

Tradition has it that in Holland St Nicholas always left a small cake, or Koekje, in the children's stockings on Christmas Eve, and it is not too difficult to see how the modern name 'cookie' came to be used to describe biscuits. Biscuits may be made by any of the methods used for making cakes; it is important to make the dough as stiff as possible, to ensure a crisp, crumbly texture.

Scotch shortbread

cooking time   30–40 minutes

you will need:

6 oz. plain flour	2 oz. castor sugar
2 oz. cornflour	½ egg yolk
4 oz. butter	

1 Sieve the flour and cornflour into a bowl.
2 Rub in the butter, add the sugar.
3 Stir in the egg yolk and work all well together.
4 Turn mixture on to a floured surface and knead well, until mixture is smooth and free from cracks.
5 Shape mixture into a round cake. Mark all round the edge with the back of a fork. Prick the centre lightly with a fork.
6 Bake in a slow oven 335°F.—Mark 3.
7 Lift carefully on to a wire tray, sprinkle with castor sugar and leave until cool.

Shortbread fingers

Make mixture as above. Roll out into an oblong. Cut into fingers and prick down the centre of each. Place on a baking tray and bake for 15–20 minutes at 350°F.—Mark 4. Cool on a wire tray and sprinkle with castor sugar.

Orange shortbread

cooking time   20–30 minutes

you will need:

8 oz. butter	8 oz. flour
4 oz. castor sugar	4 oz. fine semolina
finely grated rind 1 orange	1 extra tablespoon castor sugar

1 Butter a shallow tin, about 8 × 12 inches.
2 Cream the butter, sugar and orange rind until light and fluffy.
3 Stir in the sieved flour and semolina, mixing quickly and lightly.
4 Turn the mixture into the prepared tin, pat out smoothly to an even thickness.
5 Prick well and mark into squares or finger lengths.
6 Dust with castor sugar and bake at 335°F.— Mark 3, until lightly golden.
7 Cut into shapes and remove carefully.
8 When cold, store in an airtight tin.

Norfolk shortbreads

cooking time   15–20 minutes

you will need:

5 oz. flour	4 oz. butter or margarine
2 oz. fine semolina	2 oz. sugar
pinch salt	

1 Sieve flour, semolina and salt.
2 Cream butter and sugar until fluffy, then stir in dry ingredients.
3 Knead together lightly, turn out on to a floured board and roll out to ¼ inch in thickness. Cut into rounds with a 2-inch biscuit cutter and prick with a fork.
4 Bake on lightly greased baking trays in a moderate oven, 350°F.—Gas Mark 4, until pale golden in colour.
5 Sprinkle with castor sugar, then cool on a wire tray.
Lemon shortbread crescents Add the grated rind of 1 lemon to the creamed butter and sugar mixture. Cut into crescent shapes.
Almond shortbread triangles Reduce flour to 4 oz. and add 2 oz. ground almonds and a few drops of almond essence to the creamed butter and sugar mixture. Cut into triangles.
Chocolate shortbread fingers Sift ½ oz. cocoa powder with the dry ingredients and add a few drops of vanilla essence to the creamed butter and sugar mixture. Cut into fingers.

Lemon shortcake

cooking time   30–40 minutes

you will need:

4 oz. butter
4 oz. sugar
1 egg
4 oz. self-raising flour

4 oz. plain flour
½ teaspoon lemon juice
lemon curd

1 Sieve the flours together in a bowl.
2 Cream the fat and sugar, adding the lemon juice.
3 Beat in the egg and add the flour, working the mixture to a smooth dough.
4 Divide the mixture into two. Roll each piece into a 7-inch square.
5 Place one square on a greased and floured tray or baking tin.
6 Spread this square with lemon curd to within ½ inch of the edge.
7 Cover with the second piece. Press the edges together and 'crimp' between the fingers.
8 Bake at 350°F.—Mark 4.
9 Leave on tray until cold, sprinkle with castor sugar, and cut into fingers.

Viennese shortcakes

cooking time   20 minutes

you will need:

4 oz. self-raising flour
4 oz. plain flour
7 oz. butter

2 oz. icing sugar
½ teaspoon vanilla essence
butter cream (see page 33)

1 Grease two baking sheets.
2 Sieve both the flours together into a bowl.
3 Cream fat and sugar, adding vanilla essence.
4 Beat in the flour, working the mixture with a wooden spoon until smooth.
5 Put mixture into a forcing bag fitted with a large rose nozzle.
6 Pipe mixture in circles or strips on to the trays.
7 Bake in a moderately hot oven 375°F.—Mark 5.
8 Cool on a wire tray. When cold sandwich with butter cream.

Viennese fingers

Make as above, piping the mixture in strips about 2½ inches long. Sandwich the cold biscuits with butter cream and dip the ends in melted chocolate.

Viennese tartlets

Cut out rounds of plain biscuit mixture. Using a small nozzle, pipe Viennese shortcake mixture in a circle around the edge of each biscuit round. Bake in a moderately hot oven 375°F. —Mark 5, for 25–30 minutes. Fill the centre of the cold tartlets with lemon curd or raspberry jam. Dust with icing sugar.

Honeybee biscuits

cooking time   10–15 minutes

you will need:

4 oz. butter
2 level tablespoons honey
¼ teaspoon vanilla essence

4 oz. plain flour
chopped glacé cherries or
    chopped roasted almonds

1 Cream butter and honey until light and fluffy, add vanilla essence and mix well. Add sieved flour gradually.
2 Flour hands and roll small amounts of mixture into balls of three sizes.
3 Place three balls together, one under the other, on a greased baking sheet to form one biscuit.
4 Flatten slightly and sprinkle with chopped cherries or almonds.
5 Bake in a moderately hot oven, 375°F.— Mark 5, cool on a wire tray.

Chocolate kisses

cooking time   15 minutes

you will need:

4 oz. butter
1 oz. icing sugar
3½ oz. flour

1 dessertspoon cocoa
vanilla butter cream (see
    page 33)

1 Sieve flour and cocoa.
2 Cream the fat and sugar.
3 Gradually beat in the flour and cocoa.
4 Put mixture into a forcing bag fitted with a large star nozzle.
5 Pipe in whirls on a greased baking sheet.
6 Bake in a moderately hot oven 375°F.— Mark 5.
7 Cool on a wire tray.
8 When cold, sandwich together in pairs with butter cream.

Tea-time biscuits

cooking time   15–20 minutes

you will need:

8 oz. self-raising flour	1 egg yolk
3 oz. butter	grated rind ½ lemon
3 oz. sugar	approximately 1 tablespoon water

1 Sieve the flour.
2 Cream the fat and sugar, beat in the lemon rind and egg yolk.
3 Work in the flour, adding enough water to make a soft, pliable dough.
4 Roll out on a lightly floured surface about ⅛-inch thick.
5 Cut out into rounds or fancy shapes with cutters.
6 Bake in a moderately hot oven 375°F.—Mark 5.
7 Lift carefully on to a wire tray with a palette knife and leave until cold and crisp.
8 Dredge with castor sugar or coat with glacé icing (see page 34). Decorate with piped butter cream (see page 33), glacé cherries and walnuts, etc.

Easter cakes or biscuits

cooking time   15–20 minutes

you will need:

10 oz. flour	1 teaspoon sherry (optional)
4 oz. butter	2 oz. currants
4 oz. sugar	egg white
2 egg yolks	castor sugar

1 Sieve the flour.
2 Cream the fat and sugar, beat in egg yolks. Add the sherry, if used, and stir in the currants.
3 Work in the flour, using the hand or a palette knife, adding a little milk if necessary to make a soft dough.
4 Roll the dough out on a floured surface, cut into rounds with a fluted cutter, about 2 inches in diameter.
5 Place on a greased baking sheet and bake in a hot oven 400°F.—Mark 6.
6 After 10 minutes, remove from the oven, brush with egg white and dredge with castor sugar.
7 Return to the oven for the remaining cooking time.
8 Remove the biscuits carefully and place on a wire tray until crisp.

Sugar biscuits

cooking time   15–20 minutes

you will need:

6 oz. self-raising flour	4 oz. sugar
pinch salt	1 egg
1 oz. cornflour	vanilla essence
4 oz. butter	

1 Sieve flour, salt and cornflour into a bowl.
2 Rub in the butter and add the sugar.
3 Beat the egg with a few drops of essence and stir into the flour.
4 Work to a firm dough. Roll out on a floured surface and cut into fancy shapes.
5 Place on a baking sheet and bake at 375°F.—Mark 5.
6 Leave on a wire tray to cool. Dust with castor sugar.

Chocolate biscuits

Make as above. Sprinkle the hot biscuits with grated chocolate and leave on a wire tray to cool and set.

Orange or lemon biscuits

Make as above, adding a little finely-grated orange or lemon rind to the sieved flour. Coat the cold biscuits with orange or lemon glacé icing (see page 35).

Spicy biscuits

Make as above, adding ½ teaspoon mixed spice to the flour before sieving. Coat the cold biscuits with white glacé icing (see page 34) and decorate with a slice of preserved ginger.

Black-eyed Susans

Make dough as above, roll out barely ¼-inch thick. Cut out with round fluted cutters. Cut a small hole in the centre of half the biscuits. Place these rounds on the whole biscuits, first brushing the bases with a little egg white or water. Place on a baking sheet and bake in a moderately hot oven 375°F.—Mark 5, for 18–20 minutes. When cold, fill the centre of each with blackcurrant jam or jelly, or melted chocolate.

Lemon fingers

cooking time   20–25 minutes

you will need:

4 oz. luxury margarine   4 oz. flour
2 oz. castor sugar   lemon curd

1 Place the margarine and sugar in a mixing bowl.
2 Sieve flour into the fat and sugar.
3 Beat all together until soft and creamy with a wooden spoon—about 2 minutes.
4 Spread mixture into a Swiss roll tin. Mark in lines across surface, using the back of a fork.
5 Bake near the top of a moderate oven 350°F. —Mark 4.
6 While hot, cut into fingers and lift carefully on to a wire tray with a palette knife.
7 When cold, sandwich with lemon curd and dust with icing sugar.

Australian biscuits

cooking time   10–12 minutes

you will need:

4 oz. honey   1 egg
4 oz. sugar   10 oz. flour
1 oz. butter   1 level teaspoon salt
½ level teaspoon ground
    ginger   **icing:**
½ level teaspoon ground
    cloves   6 oz. icing sugar, sieved
½ level teaspoon nutmeg   1 tablespoon coconut
½ level teaspoon cinnamon   2 tablespoons water
1 level teaspoon   few drops lemon essence
    bicarbonate of soda

1 Place honey and sugar in a saucepan and bring to the boil. Simmer a few minutes until clear.
2 Add butter and spices, and stir until butter is dissolved. Allow to cool.
3 Beat the egg and add the bicarbonate of soda dissolved in a little milk. Stir into the honey mixture.
4 Pour this on to the sieved flour and salt, and mix well.
5 Knead until the flour is thoroughly mixed in and the dough is smooth.
6 Allow to stand in a cool place for half an hour.
7 Roll the mixture out thinly and cut into diamond shapes.
8 Bake on a greased baking tray in a moderate oven 350°F.—Mark 4.
9 Make the icing by mixing all the icing ingredients together.
10 Allow biscuits to cool, spread with icing and leave to set.

German biscuits

cooking time   10–15 minutes

you will need:

4 oz. flour   redcurrant jelly
2½ oz. butter   white glacé icing (see
1 oz. castor sugar   page 34)
                       glacé cherries

1 Sieve the flour into a bowl. Rub in the fat and add the sugar.
2 Knead the mixture by hand until it forms a smooth dough.
3 Roll out and cut into rounds with a small cutter or wine glass.
4 Bake in a slow oven 335°F.—Mark 3, until lightly coloured.
5 Place on a wire tray until cold.
6 Spread half the biscuits with redcurrant jelly and cover with the remaining biscuits.
7 Ice the top of the biscuits with white glacé icing and place a piece of glacé cherry in the centre of each.

Coffee German biscuits

Make as above, icing with coffee glacé icing (see page 35) and placing a halved walnut in the centre of each.

Lemon German biscuits

Make as above. Sandwich together with lemon curd, ice with chocolate glacé icing (see page 35) and place a halved blanched almond in the centre of each.

Bourbon biscuits

cooking time   10–15 minutes

you will need:

6 oz. flour   a few drops vanilla essence
2 oz. cocoa   chocolate cream filling
4 oz. butter   (see pages 32, 33) or
4 oz. castor sugar   melted chocolate
1 egg yolk   castor sugar

1 Sieve the flour and cocoa.
2 Rub in the fat, until the mixture resembles breadcrumbs.
3 Stir in the sugar.
4 Add the egg yolk and the essence, and mix to a firm dough, adding a little water if necessary.
5 Roll dough out thinly and prick all over with a fork. Cut into strips 3 inches by ¾ inch.
6 Place on a greased baking tray and bake in a hot oven 400°F.—Mark 6.
7 Leave on a wire tray until cold. Sandwich together with cream filling or melted chocolate.
8 Dust each lightly with a little castor sugar.

Animal crackers

cooking time   10—12 minutes

you will need:

4 oz. self-raising flour	few drops vanilla essence
good pinch salt	1 dessertspoon beaten egg
1½ oz. butter	glacé icing (see page 34)
1½ oz. sugar	silver balls for decorating

1 Sieve the flour and salt.
2 Cream the fat and sugar, and add the essence.
3 Beat in the egg and add the flour.
4 Knead to a firm paste. Roll out on a floured surface.
5 Cut out with floured animal cutters and place on a greased baking tray.
6 Prick biscuits all over with a fork.
7 Bake at 335°F.—Mark 3 until lightly coloured. Allow to cool on the baking tray, then lift carefully on to a wire tray and leave until cold.
8 Spoon a little icing on to each biscuit and spread with the back of a teaspoon to fill the shape. Press silver balls in place for eyes.

Traffic light biscuits

cooking time   10—15 minutes

you will need:

biscuit mixture as for animal crackers (see above)	red colouring
	icing sugar, sieved
8 oz. apricot jam, sieved	
green colouring	

1 Roll out the dough about ¼-inch thick. Cut into 24 pieces, 3 inches long and 1 inch wide.
2 Using a ¾-inch cutter, cut out three circles down the centre of twelve biscuits.
3 Place all the biscuits on a greased baking tray and bake on the middle shelf at 335°F.—Mark 3.
4 When the biscuits are cold, spread the plain pieces thinly with apricot jam and dredge the cut ones with icing sugar.
5 Sandwich the biscuits together.
6 Fill up the centre hole in each biscuit with apricot jam, using a teaspoon.
7 Divide the remaining jam in half. Colour one half green and the other half red.
8 Fill the top hole of each biscuit with red jam and the bottom hole with green jam.

Ginger nuts

cooking time   15—20 minutes

you will need:

4 oz. self-raising flour	1 level dessertspoon sugar
2 level teaspoons ground ginger	½ teaspoon bicarbonate of soda
1 level teaspoon ground cinnamon	2 oz. white vegetable fat
	2 tablespoons golden syrup

1 Sieve all the dry ingredients.
2 Melt the fat and syrup over a low heat and allow to cool.
3 Stir into the dry ingredients, mixing well with a wooden spoon.
4 Take pieces, about the size of a walnut, and roll into a ball between the palms of the hands.
5 Place well apart on a greased baking tray, flatten slightly.
6 Bake at 375°F.—Mark 5.

Almond drops

Make as above, omitting spices, but add ½ teaspoon almond essence with the syrup mixture. Press half a blanched almond into the centre of each ball before baking.

Coffee-time cookies

cooking time   20 minutes

you will need:

4 oz. flour	½ a beaten egg
pinch salt	coffee glacé icing (see page 35)
2 oz. butter	
2 oz. sugar	18 walnut halves

1 Sieve the flour and salt.
2 Cream the fat and sugar, and beat in the egg.
3 Stir in the flour.
4 Turn the dough on to a lightly floured surface.
5 Roll out ¼-inch thick and cut into 2-inch rounds.
6 Place on a baking sheet. Bake in a moderate oven 350°F.—Mark 4. Cool on a wire tray.
7 When cold, coat top of each with coffee glacé icing and place a walnut half on each.

Chocolate topsies

Make as above; spread cold cookies with melted chocolate and sprinkle with desiccated coconut.

Snow drops

Make as above; when cold, sandwich together with raspberry jam. Coat with glacé icing (see page 34) and sprinkle thickly with desiccated coconut.

Chocolate fingers

Make dough and roll out as above. Cut into fingers 2½ inches long. Bake for 20 minutes. When cold, dip ends of each biscuit in melted chocolate.

Lemon coconut cookies

cooking time   8–10 minutes

you will need:

4 oz. butter or margarine	4 oz. flour
pinch salt	½ teaspoon vanilla essence
1 oz. icing sugar	lemon cream or curd
	coconut

1 Sieve flour and salt.
2 Cream fat and sugar, adding essence.
3 Stir in flour and mix well.
4 Take 1 level dessertspoonful of dough for each cookie and form it into a ball, flatten slightly.
5 Place the cookies 1 inch apart on an ungreased baking tray.
6 Bake in a hot oven 400°F.—Mark 6, until lightly browned.
7 Cool on a wire tray.
8 Spread lemon cream or lemon curd on each cookie and sprinkle with desiccated coconut.

Lemon cream

Beat 1 egg slightly in a basin, over a small pan of hot water. Add the finely grated rind of 1 lemon, 6 oz. castor sugar, 3 tablespoons lemon juice and 1½ tablespoons butter. Stir and cook over hot water until well blended and thick. Allow to cool.

Chocolate orange cookies

Make as above. Top the cookies with orange flavoured glacé icing (see page 35) and sprinkle with grated chocolate. Leave in a cool place until dry.

Almond cookies

Make as above, replacing vanilla with almond essence. Press ½ a blanched almond in the centre of each cookie before baking.

Favourite cookies

Make as above, replacing vanilla with lemon essence. Coat cookies with thick white glacé icing (see page 34) and place a halved glacé cherry in the centre of each. Leave in a cool place to dry.

Chocolate chip cookies

cooking time   10 minutes

you will need:

6 oz. flour	1 oz. brown sugar
¼ teaspoon salt	1 egg
3 oz. butter	vanilla essence
3 oz. granulated sugar	4 oz. plain chocolate

1 Sieve the flour and salt.
2 Cream the fat and sugars. Beat in the essence and egg.
3 Grate or chop the chocolate coarsely and stir it into the creamed mixture with the flour.
4 Put in teaspoonfuls on a greased baking sheet and bake in a moderate oven 350°F.—Mark 4.
5 Place on a wire tray and leave until cold.

Wine cookies

cooking time   15–20 minutes

you will need:

4 oz. self-raising flour	pinch salt
4 oz. margarine	2 tablespoons sherry
2½ oz. sugar	4 oz. chopped almonds
2 egg yolks	

1 Sieve the flour and salt into a bowl.
2 Cream the fat and sugar, beat in the egg, adding a little of the flour.
3 Mix in the rest of the flour alternately with the sherry.
4 Place the chopped almonds on a plate. Drop dessertspoons of the mixture on to the almonds, toss well and roll in the palms of the hands to form small balls.
5 Place well apart on a greased baking sheet.
6 Bake in a hot oven 400°F.—Mark 6. Remove carefully on to a wire tray and leave until cold.

Press cookies

cooking time   15–20 minutes

you will need:

4 oz. flour	4 oz. sugar
2 oz. cornflour	1 egg
4 oz. butter	glacé cherries (optional)

1 Sieve the flour and cornflour.
2 Cream the fat and sugar. Beat in the egg.
3 Fold in the flour.
4 Put the mixture into a cookie press and pipe out on to a greased tray.
5 Bake in a moderate oven 350°F.—Mark 4, until lightly coloured.

The cookies may be decorated with a halved glacé cherry before baking, or, when cold, sandwiched together with strawberry cream.

Strawberry cream

Cream 1 rounded tablespoon butter with 1 tablespoon strawberry jam. Gradually work in 6 oz. sieved icing sugar. Add a few drops red colouring, if liked.

Easter cinnamon cookies

cooking time   about 15 minutes

you will need:

2 oz. castor sugar	1 rounded teaspoon
2 oz. rolled oats	ground cinnamon
4 oz. butter or margarine	white glacé icing (see
4 oz. flour	page 34)
	lemon curd

1 Place the sugar, oats, flour, cinnamon and butter in a mixing bowl, and knead until the mixture forms a ball.
2 Roll out on a well-floured surface and cut out into egg shapes, using a piece of cardboard as a guide.
3 Cut a small oval or circle from the centre of half the biscuits, using a small cutter.
4 Place on a baking sheet and bake in a moderately hot oven 375°F.—Mark 5.
5 Allow to become cool on a wire tray.
6 Cover the whole biscuits with lemon curd.
7 Coat the biscuits with the centres removed with white glacé icing.
8 Allow icing to set, then sandwich the biscuits together, placing the iced biscuits on top of the whole biscuits, giving the appearance of eggs with the whites and yolks showing.

Giant currant cookies

cooking time   10–15 minutes

you will need:

4 oz. self-raising flour	grated rind 1 orange
4 oz. fine semolina	2–4 oz. currants
4 oz. butter	2 eggs
4 oz. castor sugar	about 1 teaspoon milk

1 Sieve flour and semolina.
2 Rub in the butter until the mixture looks like fine crumbs.
3 Add sugar, orange rind and currants.
4 Stir in the beaten eggs and milk, mixing to a stiff dough.
5 Turn on to a well floured surface and knead lightly.
6 Roll out thinly and cut into rounds with a large biscuit cutter—about 3 inches.
7 Place on a buttered tray and bake in a moderately hot oven 375°F.—Mark 5, until crisp and golden.

Coconut rockies

cooking time   10–12 minutes

you will need:

4 oz. margarine	pinch salt
4 oz. sugar	3 oz. desiccated coconut
5 oz. self-raising flour	1 small egg

1 Sieve the flour and salt.
2 Cream fat and sugar, and beat in the egg.
3 Stir in the flour and coconut.
4 Half fill small paper cases with the mixture.
5 Place on a baking sheet and bake in a hot oven 425°F.—Mark 7.
6 Cool on a wire tray.

Brandy snaps

cooking time   7–10 minutes

you will need:

2 oz. flour	1 teaspoon brandy or rum
$\frac{1}{2}$ teaspoon ground ginger	essence
2 oz. butter or margarine	$\frac{1}{2}$ teaspoon grated lemon
2 oz. sugar	rind
2 tablespoons golden syrup	$\frac{1}{4}$ pint double cream

1 Grease two baking sheets.
2 Sieve flour and ginger.
3 Melt fat, sugar and syrup over a gentle heat until sugar has dissolved.
4 Remove from heat, beat in flour and flavouring.
5 Drop in teaspoonfuls 2 inches apart on a tray.
6 Bake in a moderate oven 350°F.—Mark 4.
7 Meanwhile, grease two or three wooden spoon handles.
8 Remove tray from oven and leave in a warm place so that the snaps cool without becoming too hard.
9 Remove from the tray one at a time, using a palette knife, and roll round a wooden spoon. Leave in a cool place until firm. Slip carefully off handle.
10 Shape each in the same way and pipe whisked double cream into the end of each.
11 If snaps become too hard to roll, pop tray back into the oven for 1–2 minutes to soften mixture.

Coconut pyramids

cooking time   3–4 hours

you will need:

2 egg whites	5 oz. desiccated coconut
5 oz. sugar	glacé cherries

1 Grease a baking sheet. Cut small rounds of rice paper, if liked, about 2 inches in diameter and place on the baking sheet.
2 Whisk egg whites stiffly and fold in sugar and coconut. Tint half the mixture pink, if liked.
3 Pile mixture on rounds of paper or on to the baking sheet. Form into pyramid shapes.
4 Bake in a slow oven 265°F.—Mark ½, until touched with gold. Top each with a glacé cherry, halved, half way through the cooking time.
5 Cool on a wire tray. Trim rice paper if necessary.

Chocolate coconut pyramids

Make as above, omitting cherries. Allow the pyramids to cool and then top each with a teaspoon melted chocolate. Allow chocolate to run down the sides a little and set.

Macaroons

cooking time   20–25 minutes

you will need:

2 egg whites	1 teaspoon orange flower
4 oz. ground almonds	water (optional, obtain-
8 oz. castor sugar	able from chemists)
1 oz. ground rice	blanched whole almonds
	egg white, to glaze

1 Whisk the egg whites until stiff.
2 Stir in the ground almonds, sugar, ground rice and orange flower water. Mix well.
3 Grease a baking tray and cover with a sheet of rice paper.
4 Spoon the mixture on to the tray in little heaps, leaving space between each, to allow biscuits to spread.
5 Place a split blanched almond in the centre of each and brush the almond with egg white.
6 Bake in a moderate oven 350°F.—Mark 4, until pale gold in colour.
7 Leave on the tray until firm, then cut round each biscuit, trimming the rice paper neatly. Place on a wire tray until cold.

Chocolate macaroons

Make as above, omitting the almond decoration.
Coat the finished biscuits with melted chocolate.

Pralines

cooking time   10–15 minutes

you will need:

6 oz. self-raising flour	1 egg
4 oz. margarine	½ teaspoon vanilla essence
6 oz. brown sugar	3 oz. chopped nuts

1 Cream fat and sugar, and add the essence. Beat in the egg.
2 Stir in the flour and nuts.
3 Roll the mixture between the palms of the hands to form 1-inch balls.
4 Place well apart on a baking sheet. Flatten each ball until about ¼ inch thick.
5 Bake in a moderately hot oven 375°F.—Mark 5.
6 Cool on a wire tray.

Marzipan petits fours

cooking time   20–30 minutes

you will need:

4 oz. ground almonds	2 egg yolks
4 oz. castor sugar	cherries, angelica or halved
almond essence	walnuts

1 Grease a baking tray lightly and cover with a piece of rice paper.
2 Mix the almonds, sugar and a few drops of almond essence.
3 Stir in sufficient egg yolk to bind to a stiff paste.
4 Turn the paste on to a surface dusted with castor sugar, dredge with more castor sugar and roll out about ½ inch thick.
5 Cut into small fancy shapes and decorate with halved glacé cherries, walnuts or pieces of angelica. Place on the prepared tray.
6 Bake in a slow oven 310°F.—Mark 2, until lightly coloured and firm to the touch.
7 Allow to become cold on the tray. Cut rice paper to the shape of each cake.

Cheese straws

cooking time   10–15 minutes

you will need:

4 oz. flour	1 egg yolk
2 oz. butter or margarine	salt and pepper
2 oz. finely grated Cheddar	cayenne, if liked
cheese	pinch dry mustard

1 Sieve flour and seasonings. Rub in fat.
2 Add cheese and yolk of egg.
3 Mix all together with just enough water to make a stiff dough.
4 Roll out ¼-inch thick and cut into strips 3 inches long and ¼-inch square. Bake at 400°F.—Mark 6 until golden brown.

Cakes from Abroad

Warm spicy coffee cake, croissants and black cherry jam, cheese cake topped with sun ripened peaches—haven't you often wished when you returned from holiday that you could enjoy again some of those delicious cakes and pastries you tried abroad? Here are some you'll want to make at home.

Chestnut tarts (Israel)

cooking time   15–20 minutes

you will need:

6 oz. shortcrust pastry	1 tablespoon sherry
apricot jam	4 oz. castor sugar
6 oz. chestnuts	1 egg

1 Roll pastry out thinly and use to line some patty tins. Prick the pastry well.
2 Spread with jam.
3 Cut off the end of each chestnut with a sharp knife.
4 Cook in fast boiling water for 15 minutes. Drain, peel and run through a sieve.
5 Blend with the sherry, sugar and egg.
6 Put a good spoonful of the mixture into each patty case.
7 Bake in a hot oven 400°F.—Mark 6, until the pastry is cooked.
8 When cold, dust with icing sugar, or coat with a little glacé icing (see page 34).

Butter cookies (Holland)

cooking time   10–15 minutes

you will need:

8 oz. flour	1 egg
4 oz. butter	blanched almonds
4 oz. Demerara sugar	

1 Sieve the flour.
2 Cream the butter and sugar. Stir in the flour.
3 Mix to a dough with the beaten egg.
4 Knead lightly and roll out on a floured surface.
5 Cut into rounds and press a halved almond on each.
6 Bake in a moderate oven 350°F.—Mark 4, until lightly coloured.

Austrian almond slices

cooking time   35–40 minutes

you will need:

8 oz. short-crust pastry	3 oz. ground almonds
4 oz. butter	few drops almond essence
4 oz. sugar	apricot jam

1 Roll out the pastry and use to line a Swiss roll tin, 11 × 7 inches. Prick the bottom with a fork and spread thinly with apricot jam.
2 Melt the butter over a gentle heat. Stir in the sugar, almonds and essence.
3 Spread the filling evenly over the jam.
4 Bake in a moderate oven 350°F.—Mark 4.
5 Cut into sixteen slices while still warm. Lift each out carefully and cool on a wire tray.

French apricot tarts

cooking time   15–20 minutes

you will need:

6 oz. shortcrust pastry	1 small can apricot halves
French cream filling (see page 34)	2 tablespoons apricot glaze (see page 37)

1 Roll pastry out thinly and cut into 12 rounds, large enough to line patty tins. Prick the bottoms lightly with a fork.
2 Fill each pastry case with cold French cream filling. Place a drained apricot half, cut side down, on top of the filling in each tartlet.
3 Bake in a moderately hot oven 375°F.—Mark 5.
4 Remove from the oven, brush the top of each with hot apricot glaze.
5 Leave on a wire tray until cold.

Neapolitan cakes

cooking time   20 minutes

you will need:

4 oz. flour	1 egg
pinch salt	apricot jam
4 oz. butter	glacé icing (see page 34)
4 oz. sugar	glacé cherries
4 oz. ground almonds	

1 Sieve flour and salt into a bowl.
2 Rub in the fat, add the sugar and almonds.
3 Stir in the egg and mix to a stiff paste.
4 Roll out $\frac{1}{8}$ inch thick and cut into rounds with a $2\frac{1}{2}$-inch cutter.
5 Bake on a greased baking sheet in a moderately hot oven 375°F.—Mark 5.
6 Leave until cold. Spread half the rounds with jam. Press the other rounds firmly on top.
7 Ice the tops with glacé icing and place half a cherry in the centre of each.

Russian cake
you will need:

2 thin 7-inch squares of sponge or Victoria sandwich cake (make 1 cake, using 4 oz. flour, and cut through)	2 oz. sugar
	$\frac{1}{8}$ pint water
	rum
	thick pink glacé icing (see page 34)
apricot jam	
scraps of sponge cake to fill a shallow 7-inch tin	chocolate feather icing (see page 35)

1 Place sugar and water in a pan and boil for 10 minutes. Add rum to taste.
2 Place the scraps of cake in a bowl. Pour on the syrup.
3 Brush a 7-inch tin with melted butter.
4 Press one piece of cake into the bottom of the tin and spread with jam.
5 Cover with the moistened scraps of cake.
6 Spread the second piece of cake with jam and press, jam side down, on to the scraps of cake.
7 Place a plate and weight on the cake and leave in a cool place overnight.
8 Turn the cake out on to a board and coat top with pink glacé icing.
9 Decorate with chocolate feather icing.
10 When the icing is firmly set, cut the cake into slices with a sharp knife.

For a richer cake, the scraps of cake may be soaked with sherry instead of the sugar syrup, and almond paste (see page 37) may be used to make the top and bottom layers.

Danish strawberry cake

Make a round of shortbread (see page 62). When cold, brush with redcurrant jelly which has been dissolved over a gentle heat. Cover with strawberries, cut through and placed cut-side down on the shortbread. Brush each strawberry with more jelly. When cool, decorate with cream and blanched almonds.

Swiss chocolate cake
cooking time $1\frac{3}{4}$–2 hours

you will need:

4 oz. plain chocolate	4 eggs
4 oz. butter	4 oz. ground almonds
4 oz. icing sugar	1 oz. plain flour

1 Grease an oblong tin 8 × 6 inches. Line the bottom with greased greaseproof paper.
2 Melt the chocolate in a basin over hot water.
3 Cream the butter and sugar together and beat in the melted chocolate.
4 Separate the yolks and whites of the eggs. Beat the yolks into the creamed mixture.
5 Beat in the almonds and flour.
6 Whisk the egg whites until stiff and fold lightly

into the mixture.
7 Pour into the tin and spread evenly with a palette knife.
8 Bake on the middle shelf at 335°F.—Mark 3.
9 Turn out on to a wire tray to cool.
10 When cold, coat with chocolate icing (see page 35) and sprinkle with chopped almonds.

Drunken sponge (Spain)
you will need:

1 round sponge cake	6 oz. icing sugar
4 tablespoons sugar	$\frac{1}{4}$ pint double cream
4 tablespoons water	sliced peaches, fresh or canned
$\frac{1}{4}$ pint brandy or rum	

1 Make a syrup by boiling the sugar and water together for 5 minutes.
2 Place the sponge cake on a dish and pour on the hot sugar syrup.
3 Sprinkle the sponge with the brandy or rum and leave to soak.
4 Blend the icing sugar with a little warm water to make a thick coating consistency.
5 Pour over the top of the sponge and leave until dry.
6 Whisk the cream until thick and pile in the centre of the sponge. Arrange the sliced peaches round. If canned peaches are used, make sure they are well drained beforehand.
7 If liked, the cream may be sprinkled with coarsely grated chocolate.

Continental yeast cake
cooking time   30–40 minutes

you will need:

8 oz. flour	rind $\frac{1}{2}$ orange, minced or finely chopped
$\frac{1}{2}$ level teaspoon salt	
2 oz. fine semolina	juice $\frac{1}{2}$ orange
2 oz. sugar	2 eggs
3 oz. margarine	$\frac{1}{8}$ pint milk
1 oz. yeast	4 oz. currants

1 Grease and flour a shallow Yorkshire pudding tin—$8\frac{1}{2} \times 5\frac{1}{2}$ inches.
2 Sieve the flour and salt, add semolina and sugar.
3 Rub in the margarine. Crumble yeast between fingers and rub in.
4 Make a well in the centre and beat in the eggs and milk.
5 Add currants, orange rind and juice, and work to a soft dough with a wooden spoon.
6 Turn into the prepared tin and spread mixture evenly, using the fingers.
7 Put to rise in a warm place until double its size.
8 Bake on the top shelf at 400°F.—Mark 6. Turn on to a wire tray to cool.
9 Serve cut into fingers and spread with butter.

Orange halva cake (Greece)

cooking time 40 minutes

you will need:

9 oz. semolina
3 level teaspoons baking powder
6 oz. ground almonds
6 oz. butter
6 oz. castor sugar

1½ level teaspoons finely grated orange rind
5 tablespoons orange juice
5 eggs

syrup:

6 oz. castor sugar
5 tablespoons water
2 dessertspoons lemon juice
1½-inch piece cinnamon stick

3 tablespoons orange juice
1 tablespoon finely sliced candied orange peel

1 Grease a 9-inch ring tin.
2 Sieve semolina, baking powder and ground almonds.
3 Cream butter, sugar and orange rind. Beat in orange juice.
4 Whisk eggs and beat in gradually.
5 Fold in sieved semolina, baking powder and ground almonds. Turn mixture into prepared tin.
6 Place in hot oven, 425°F.—Mark 7, and cook for 10 minutes. Reduce heat to 355°F.—Mark 4, and cook a further 30 minutes, until the cake is firm and golden.
7 A few minutes before the cake is cooked, make a syrup of sugar, water, lemon juice and cinnamon stick. Boil, without stirring, until syrup begins to thicken but do not allow it to change colour. Add the orange juice and peel, and boil up for a second.
8 Turn the cake out on to a large warm plate. Pour the hot syrup over it at once.
9 Serve plain or with unsweetened whipped cream and toasted almonds.

Croissants

cooking time 20 minutes

you will need:

dry mix for dough:
1 lb. strong plain flour
2 level teaspoons salt
1 oz. lard, rubbed in
1 egg, beaten

yeast liquid:
1 oz. fresh yeast blended with ½ pint water, less 4 tablespoons

To make the pastry

4–6 oz. hard margarine.
Egg wash—beat an egg with a little water and ½ teaspoon sugar.

To make the dough.

1 Make a dough with the dry mix, yeast liquid and egg.
2 Knead, on a lightly floured board, until the dough is smooth, 10–15 minutes.

To make the pastry

3 Roll the dough into a long strip approximately 20×6×¼ inch thick, taking care to keep the dough piece rectangular.
4 Divide the margarine in three. Use one part to dot the dough, covering the top two-thirds of the surface, leaving a small border clear. Fold in three, by bringing up the plain part of the dough first, then bringing the top part over. Turn the dough so that the fold is on the right-hand side. Seal the edges by pressing with the rolling pin. Re-shape to a long strip by gently pressing the dough at intervals with the rolling pin. Again, take care to keep the dough piece rectangular.
5 Repeat with the other two portions of margarine.
6 Place in an oiled polythene bag and allow to rise in the refrigerator for 30 minutes.
7 Roll out, as before, to a rectangular strip. Repeat folding and rolling three times more. Place in a refrigerator for at least 1 hour. The dough can be stored overnight in the refrigerator at this stage or up to 3 days, ready to make croissants at any time.

To shape the croissants

8 Roll the dough to a rectangle slightly larger than 21×12 inches. Cover with greased polythene and leave 10 minutes.
9 Trim edges with a sharp knife, and divide in half lengthwise. Cut each strip into six triangles 6 inches high, with a 6-inch base. Brush with egg wash. Roll up each triangle loosely, towards point, finishing with the tip underneath. Curve into crescent shape.
10 After shaping, put croissants on ungreased sheet. Brush tops with egg wash, put inside a lightly oiled polythene bag and leave at room temperature for about 30 minutes until light and puffy. Brush again with egg wash before baking.
11 Bake on the middle shelf of oven at 425°F.—Mark 7.
12 Croissants are best served warm.

Savarin (France)

cooking time   25–30 minutes

you will need:

½ oz. yeast	5 oz. butter, melted
1 teaspoon sugar	chopped blanched almonds
¼ pint tepid milk	rum or brandy syrup
8 oz. flour	glacé cherries and blanched
1 teaspoon salt	almonds
4 eggs	whipped cream (optional)

1 Cream the yeast and sugar, stir in the milk and leave in a warm place for 5 minutes.
2 Sieve the flour and salt into a large bowl. Make a well in the centre and pour in the yeast mixture. Spoon some of the flour over the yeast so that it is covered. Leave in a warm place for about 1 hour.
3 Add the beaten eggs and melted butter, and beat well, using the hands.
4 Brush a ring mould 8 inches in diameter with melted butter. Sprinkle with chopped nuts. Pour in the batter to half fill the ring mould.
5 Leave in a warm place until the batter doubles its size and fills the mould.
6 Bake in a moderately hot oven 375°F.—Mark 5, until golden and firm to the touch.
7 Turn out and leave until cold. Place on a serving dish, pour on the rum syrup and decorate with almonds and cherries. Pipe with cream, if liked.

Rum or brandy syrup

Boil 4 oz. sugar and ¼ pint water together for 10 minutes. Add rum or brandy to taste.

Honey cheese cake (International)

cooking time   40 minutes

you will need:

pastry:

4 oz. flour	12 oz. cottage cheese
2 oz. fine semolina	3 eggs
pinch salt	1 tablespoon honey
3 oz. butter	1 tablespoon fine semolina
½ oz. castor sugar	3 tablespoons double
cold water	cream
	1 tablespoon lemon juice
	1 tablespoon castor sugar
	1 teaspoon ground
	cinnamon

filling:
3 tablespoons chopped dates, raisins or sultanas
1 tablespoon mixed peel

1 Make pastry by sifting flour, semolina and salt into a bowl.
2 Rub in the fat and add the sugar.
3 Mix to a stiff dough with water.
4 Line an 8-inch flan ring or 10-inch pie plate.

5 Sprinkle fruit lightly over the bottom of the pastry case.
6 Sieve cheese into a large bowl. Blend in egg yolks, honey, semolina, cream and lemon juice.
7 Whisk egg whites until stiff, fold into the mixture.
8 Pour into flan, sprinkle with sugar and cinnamon.
9 Bake in a hot oven 400°F.—Mark 6, for 10 minutes. Reduce heat to moderate 350°F.—Mark 4 and bake for a further 30 minutes.
10 Allow to cool before removing from flan ring.

Swedish tea bread

cooking time   30–35 minutes

you will need:

batter:

2 oz. flour	1 tablespoon oil
½ teaspoon castor sugar	1 egg, well beaten
¼ oz. fresh yeast or 1 level	
teaspoon dried yeast	**filling:**
4 fluid oz. warm milk	½ oz. butter, melted
	3 oz. brown sugar
other ingredients:	2 level teaspoons cinnamon
6 oz. flour	glacé icing (see page 34)
½ teaspoon salt	glacé cherries, chopped
	nuts, chopped

1 Blend the batter ingredients together in a large bowl. Leave for 20–30 minutes until the mixture froths.
2 Add the flour, salt, oil and egg, and mix well.
3 Knead the dough thoroughly for about 10 minutes on a lightly floured surface.
4 Put to rise in a lightly oiled polythene bag, loosely tied, until the dough springs back when pressed gently with a floured finger—about 1–2 hours.
5 Roll the risen dough to a rectangle, about 12 × 9 inches.
6 Brush with melted butter. Sprinkle with brown sugar and cinnamon.
7 Roll up tightly, beginning with the wide side, and seal the edges. Bring the ends together to form a ring, seal and place on a baking tray, lightly greased.
8 With scissors, cut slashes 1 inch apart to within ½ inch of the centre. Turn the cut sections on their sides.
9 Put the tray inside a lightly oiled polythene bag and leave to rise in a cool place until the dough feels springy.
10 Remove the bag and bake on the middle shelf of a moderate oven 350°F.—Mark 4.
11 Cool on a wire tray.
12 When cold, ice with glacé icing and decorate with chopped glacé cherries and nuts.

Favorki-Chrust (Poland)

you will need:

8 oz. flour	2 oz. sugar
2 oz. butter	½ teaspoon bicarbonate of
3 egg yolks	soda
1 whole egg	¼ pint single cream
	salt

Rub the fat into the flour, add the other ingredients and mix to a smooth paste. Roll out thinly, cut into strips 4 inches long and 1 inch wide. Make a slit at one end of each strip and push the other end through it. Fry quickly in deep fat until golden brown.

Almond cake (Spain)

cooking time   15–20 minutes

you will need:

½ oz. butter	3 oz. biscuit crumbs
5 oz. sugar	6 eggs
5 oz. ground almonds	

1 Beat the yolks with the sugar until frothy.
2 Whisk the whites until stiff and fold in.
3 Add the biscuit crumbs and ground almonds and beat well.
4 Pour the mixture into a well buttered baking tin.
5 Bake in a moderate oven 350°F.—Mark 4.

Anzacs (Australia)

cooking time   15 minutes

you will need:

4 oz. flour	½ teaspoon baking powder
4 oz. rolled oats	1 tablespoon golden syrup
4 oz. desiccated coconut	4 oz. butter, melted
4 oz. sugar	

1 Mix all the dry ingredients together.
2 Stir in the syrup and the melted butter.
3 Roll into small balls and flatten slightly.
4 Place on a greased baking tray.
5 Bake in a cool oven 310°F.—Mark 2.
6 Cool on a wire tray.

Bishop's bread (Austria)

cooking time   1 hour

you will need:

4 oz. butter	4 oz. flour
4 oz. sugar	1 cup mixed chopped
5 egg whites	citron peel, sultanas
5 egg yolks	orange rind and roughly
rind and juice 1 lemon	chopped chocolate

1 Cream the butter and sugar.
2 Add the egg yolks well beaten, one at a time.

3 Beat very well and add the lemon juice.
4 Mix all the dry ingredients together (flour, peel, etc.).
5 Whisk the egg whites until stiff.
6 Fold the flour mixture and the whites of eggs alternately into the butter mixture.
7 Pour into a well-greased deep cake-tin with a loose base. Bake in a moderate oven 350°F.—Mark 4.

Borrachitos (Spain)

cooking time   10–15 minutes

you will need:

3½ oz. butter	5 oz. flour
2 oz. sugar	1 teaspoon baking powder
1 teaspoon vanilla essence	sugar to glaze
3 eggs	

1 Cream the butter with the sugar, add the vanilla essence.
2 Beat the yolks and mix with the flour and baking powder.
3 Whisk the whites until stiff and fold in, mixing well.
4 Pour the batter into small greased patty tins or paper cases.
5 Bake in a hot oven 400°F.—Mark 6.
6 Allow to cool and pour sugar syrup over them.

Boomerang cake (Australia)

cooking time   about 40 minutes

you will need:

5 oz. self-raising flour	**icing:**
4 oz. butter	6 oz. icing sugar
2 level tablespoons coconut	1 level tablespoon cocoa
2 level tablespoons cocoa	3 oz. butter
8 oz. sugar	1 teaspoon coffee essence
2 eggs	few drops vanilla essence
pinch salt	1 tablespoon coconut
3 tablespoons milk	
few drops vanilla essence	

1 Cream together butter, coconut, cocoa and sugar, then add the eggs gradually, beating well.
2 Sieve the flour and salt and beat it in alternately with the milk and vanilla essence.
3 Line the bottom of a greased 7-inch cake tin, pour in the mixture and bake in a moderate oven 350°F.—Mark 4.
4 To make icing, sieve icing sugar and mix with cocoa, melt the butter and add to the sugar with the coffee and vanilla essence.
5 Beat until the icing is smooth.
6 Spread on to the cake when cold, and pull the top into peaks. Sprinkle with coconut.

Botercake (Holland)

cooking time   1½ hours

you will need:

8 oz. unsalted butter	4 eggs
8 oz. self-raising flour	5 oz. dried fruit
8 oz. castor sugar	

1 Cream the butter and sugar.
2 Beat in the beaten eggs, a little at a time, keeping the mixture stiff.
3 Fold in sieved flour and the fruit.
4 Turn mixture into a greased loaf tin and bake in a slow oven 335°F.—Mark 3 until golden brown.

Danish Christmas biscuits

cooking time   15–20 minutes

you will need:

4 oz. plain flour	1¾ teaspoons cinnamon
3 oz. butter	pinch salt
4 oz. castor sugar	blanched almonds to
1 large egg	decorate

1 Save white of egg, 1 oz. of sugar and 1 teaspoon of the cinnamon for glazing.
2 Rub butter into the flour with the finger tips till mixture is like fine breadcrumbs.
3 Add egg yolk, sugar, salt and the spice.
4 Mix dough with a wooden spoon and knead lightly until smooth.
5 Roll out dough ¼ inch thick. Cut out biscuits with a 1½-inch pastry cutter.
6 Brush the top of the biscuits with the egg white to which 1 oz. sugar and 1 teaspoon of the spice has been added.
7 Place 1 blanched almond on each biscuit. Bake on a lightly greased tray in a slow oven 335°F. —Mark 3 until golden.

Hazelnut biscuits (Spain)

cooking time   about 15 minutes

you will need:

8 oz. ground hazelnuts	1 tablespoon grated lemon
1 egg	rind
2 oz. flour	juice ½ lemon
	3 oz. castor sugar

1 Pound the hazelnuts with the sugar to a fine paste, add the flour and lemon rind.
2 Beat the egg and lemon juice together and add to the mixture.
3 Place teaspoonfuls on a greased baking sheet.
4 Bake in a moderate oven 350°F.—Mark 4 until the biscuits are brown and crisp.

Genoa cake

cooking time   1½ hours

you will need:

8 oz. self-raising flour	grated rind 1 lemon
6 oz. butter	3 oz. glacé cherries
6 oz. sugar	3 oz. mixed chopped peel
4 eggs	extra sugar for decorating

1 Grease and line an 8-inch tin.
2 Sieve the flour.
3 Cream the fat and sugar, adding the lemon rind.
4 Beat in the eggs.
5 Chop the cherries, mix with the peel and stir into the flour.
6 Fold flour into the creamed mixture.
7 Turn into the prepared tin and sprinkle the top with sugar.
8 Bake in a moderate oven 350°F.—Mark 4.
9 Turn out on to a wire tray to cool.

Honey and nut roll (Spain)

cooking time   25–30 minutes

you will need:

pastry:	filling:
8 oz. flour	honey
4 oz. butter	chopped walnuts and
pinch salt	hazelnuts
1 tablespoon castor sugar	chopped candied peel
1 egg yolk	castor sugar
½ glass sherry	
1 tablespoon lemon juice	

1 Rub the butter into the flour, add salt and sugar, beaten egg yolk, lemon juice and sherry to make into a stiff paste. If necessary add a little cold water.
2 Roll into a strip. Brush with honey and sprinkle with chopped nuts and chopped candied peel.
3 Roll up and sprinkle with a little castor sugar.
4 Bake in a moderate oven 350°F.—Mark 4 until golden.
5 Cut into slices when cold.

Jewish krack-a-jack

cooking time   about 1 hour

you will need:

8 oz. rolled oats	1 teaspoon almond essence
4 oz. butter or margarine	½ teaspoon bicarbonate of
4 oz. brown sugar	soda
	castor sugar

1 Melt the fat and sugar in saucepan over gentle heat.
2 Add oats, essence and soda dissolved in a little warm water. Mix well.
3 Spread in a greased shallow tin.
4 Bake in a moderately hot oven 375°F.— Mark 5.
5 When cool, cut into pieces and dust with castor sugar.

Honey wafer cake (Czechoslovakia)

cooking time   about 10 minutes

you will need:

8 oz. plain flour	chopped nuts or chocolate
1 egg	to decorate
3 oz. sugar	
1 oz. butter	**filling:**
1 teaspoon bicarbonate of	1 pint milk
soda	3 oz. sugar
1 tablespoon honey	1 tablespoon cocoa
few drops vanilla essence	2 oz. butter
	1 oz. cornflour

1 Whisk the honey, sugar, egg, vanilla and butter to a thick cream over a saucepan of boiling water.
2 Add the soda and after whisking for a little while longer remove from the heat and fold in the flour.
3 When cool turn on to a floured board.
4 Divide into five parts and roll out each to wafer thinness.
5 Bake in a moderate oven 350°F.—Mark 4 on greased baking trays.
6 When golden remove from the oven. Using a knife, remove from the tray while still warm.
7 Mix a little of the milk for the cream filling with the cornflour.
8 Bring the rest of the milk to the boil, add the cornflour and stir. Boil for a few minutes, then remove from the heat. Add sugar.
9 When cold add the butter and cocoa.
10 Sandwich the wafers with the cream filling, cover with a weight and leave for several hours in a cool place.
11 Decorate with the remaining cream, sprinkle with toasted chopped nuts or grated chocolate.

Jewish sand cake

cooking time   1 hour 40 minutes

you will need:

8 oz. butter	6 oz. cornflour
8 oz. castor sugar	2 oz. plain flour
4 eggs	

1 Sieve flour and cornflour.
2 Melt butter in saucepan over gentle heat.
3 Separate yolks and whites of eggs.
4 Whisk whites until stiff, add sugar and beat for 1 minute.
5 Add yolks and beat for a further 2 minutes.
6 Gradually fold in flour and cornflour, alternately with cooled, melted butter.
7 Pour into well greased 8-inch tin and bake in a moderate oven 350°F.—Mark 4.

Lamingtons (New Zealand)

cooking time   50–60 minutes

you will need:

5 oz. butter	raspberry jam
7 oz. sugar	
½ teaspoon vanilla essence	**icing:**
3 eggs	7 oz. icing sugar
10 oz. self-raising flour	1 oz. cocoa
pinch salt	3 tablespoons boiling water
4 tablespoons milk	6 oz. desiccated coconut

1 Cream butter and sugar, add vanilla essence.
2 Add eggs one by one and beat well.
3 Fold in sieved flour and salt alternately with the milk.
4 Pour mixture into a greased 8-inch square cake tin and bake in a moderate oven 350°F.—Mark 4.
5 Cool and store in an airtight tin.
6 Next day slit cake through centre and spread with jam.
7 Sandwich together and cut the cake into 2-inch squares.
8 To make icing, blend sieved icing sugar and cocoa and pour on the boiling water.
9 Work together with a wooden spoon, adding more water if necessary.
10 Place the icing over hot water to keep it thin, then dip the squares of cake in, using a fork to hold the cake.
11 Toss each cake in coconut, then stand on a wire cake tray to set.

Lucia cats (Sweden)

cooking time   about 20 minutes

you will need:

½ pint milk	25 almonds
6 oz. butter	5 bitter almonds
6 oz. sugar	10 tablespoons raisins
1 egg	
5 grains saffron	**glaze:**
2 oz. yeast	1 beaten egg
2 lb. flour	granulated sugar
	10 chopped almonds

1 Warm milk adding saffron.
2 Blend yeast with a little sugar.
3 Mix flour, yeast, milk and egg to smooth dough.
4 Cream butter and remaining sugar until light and creamy. Work into dough.
5 Allow to rise for 30 minutes.
6 Blanch and chop almonds finely and work into dough together with raisins.
7 Place dough on floured baking board and shape into buns.
8 Make cut on 2 opposite sides of each bun, elongate corners a little and curl outwards.

9 Place on greased baking sheet and allow to rise for 20 minutes.
10 Brush with eggs and sprinkle with sugar and chopped almonds.
11 Bake in a hot oven 450°F.—Mark 8 until golden brown.

Oat cake with apples (Sweden)

cooking time   about 40 minutes

you will need:

3 oz. sugar	6 tablespoons self-raising
3 oz. butter	flour
1 egg	6 tablespoons milk
2 oz. rolled oats	3 apples
cinnamon	sugar
	breadcrumbs

1 Grease a cake tin and sprinkle with breadcrumbs.
2 Cream butter and sugar.
3 Add egg and mix in well.
4 Stir in milk, oats and flour, a little at a time, until well mixed.
5 Pour into cake tin.
6 Peel and slice apples.
7 Dip in mixture of sugar and cinnamon and place in rings on cake.
8 Press them down a little and sprinkle some sugar and cinnamon over top.
9 Bake in moderate oven 350°F.—Mark 4.
10 Turn out while still warm and serve immediately.

Saffron buns (Russia)

cooking time   about 20 minutes

you will need:

1 lb. flour	about 1½ cups milk
1 oz. yeast	2 oz. sultanas
2 eggs	pinch saffron
6 oz. butter	¼ teaspoon salt
3 oz. sugar	2 tablespoons sugar syrup

1 Dissolve the yeast in 1 cup warm milk, mix with half the flour.
2 Cover with a cloth and leave in a warm place, to rise.
3 Cream the butter and sugar, add a beaten egg, sultanas, salt, the remaining flour and the saffron dissolved in a teaspoon of milk.
4 Combine with the yeast dough and knead until firm but not too stiff.
5 Shape into a ball, cover and leave in a warm place until double its size.

6 Roll out the dough, shape into small buns, put on to a greased tin and prove for 10 minutes.
7 Brush with milk and bake in a hot oven 425°F.—Mark 7 until brown.
8 Remove from the oven, put on to a wire cake tray and, while still hot, glaze with sugar syrup.

Tartlettes (Germany)

cooking time   10 minutes

you will need:

4 oz. sugar	4 oz. almonds
6 oz. butter	2 oz. sugar
6 oz. flour	cinnamon
2 egg yolks	nutmeg
1 egg white	lemon peel

Cream the butter with the sugar and a little grated lemon peel. Beat in the egg yolks, fold in the sifted flour. Drop small spoonfuls of the mixture on to greased baking tins. Beat the egg white with 1 tablespoon water. Brush the biscuits with it. Mix the almonds with the sugar, cinnamon and nutmeg. Sprinkle over the biscuits. Bake in a moderate oven for 10 minutes.

Stuffed monkey (South Africa)

cooking time   about 30 minutes

you will need:

8 oz. flour	**stuffing:**
6 oz. butter	2 oz. chopped lemon peel
6 oz. brown sugar	4 oz. ground almonds
1 whole egg	1½ oz. butter (melted)
1 egg white	1 egg yolk
½ teaspoon cinnamon	
¼ teaspoon salt	

1 Sieve the flour, cinnamon and salt.
2 Rub in the butter, add the sugar, mix well, add the beaten whole egg and mix to a soft dough.
3 Divide in two pieces and roll ⅛ inch thick.
4 Mix all the ingredients of the stuffing well together.
5 Pile on one piece of dough on a baking sheet, damp the edges, put the other piece of dough on top and seal the edges.
6 Brush with the egg white and cook in a moderate oven 350°F.—Mark 4.
7 Cut in squares and serve.

Spicy coffee cake (Russia)

cooking time   25 minutes

you will need:

3 oz. flour	1 egg
3 oz. fine semolina	¼ pint milk
3 level teaspoons baking	**crumble:**
powder	1 oz. flour
pinch salt	1 oz. fine semolina
1 teaspoon each cinnamon	2 teaspoons cinnamon
and ginger	1 oz. butter
2 oz. butter	1 oz. sugar
3 oz. sugar	

1 Grease a shallow 8-inch square tin.
2 Sieve flour, semolina, baking powder, salt and spices for cake.
3 Rub in the butter and add the sugar.
4 Stir in the beaten egg and milk. Turn into the tin.
5 Sieve flour, semolina and cinnamon for the crumble.
6 Rub in the butter and add the sugar.
7 Sprinkle over the cake mixture, press down lightly.
8 Bake at 400°F.—Mark 6.
  Serve hot with coffee or as a dessert with thick apple sauce or whipped cream.

French Pastries

Jalousie

1 Divide 4 oz. flaky pastry into two pieces.
2 Roll out into an oblong about 6 × 4½ inches.
3 Put one oblong on a baking tray and spread with 1 heaped tablespoon raspberry jam, leaving a ½-inch margin all round.
4 Fold the other oblong in half lengthways. Cut through the folded edge at intervals to make slits, leaving a ½-inch margin at each end of the fold.
5 Open the piece of pastry out again and damp the edge with water.
6 Place damp side down on the jam-covered pastry and seal the edges. Brush the whole pastry with water and dredge with sugar. Leave in a cold place for 10 minutes.
7 Bake in a hot oven 425°F.—Mark 7, on the second shelf from the top for 20–25 minutes.
8 Cool on a wire tray. Cut into six slices when cold.

Palmiers

1 Roll 4 oz. flaky pastry into an oblong about 8 × 14 inches.
2 Brush the pastry lightly with water. Fold the narrow edges to the centre, brush again with water.
3 Fold the pastry over again, so that the folded edges meet in the centre.
4 Cut into twelve ½-inch strips with a sharp knife. Brush the cut side of each with water and sprinkle with castor sugar.
5 Place on a baking tray, leaving space for the pastries to spread. Leave in a cold place for 10 minutes.
6 Bake in a hot oven 425°F.—Mark 7, on the second shelf from the top for 15–20 minutes. Turn the pastries over half way through the cooking time, to brown the other side.
7 Cool on a wire tray. When cold, sandwich together with whipped cream and dust with icing sugar.

Almond twists

1 Roll 4 oz. flaky pastry into an oblong 5 × 14 inches. Cut into ½-inch strips. Twist the pastry strips and place on a baking tray.
2 Brush with water and sprinkle with castor sugar. Leave in a cold place for 10 minutes.
3 Bake in a hot oven 425°F.—Mark 7, for 15–20 minutes.
4 Remove and place on a wire tray.
5 Brush the hot pastry with apricot glaze (see page 37) and sprinkle with chopped, toasted almonds. Leave until cold.

Flan à la Normande

1 Line a 7-inch flan ring with 4 oz. rich short-crust pastry.
2 Peel and core 1 lb. cooking apples. Stew with 4 oz. sugar until reduced to a pulp. Leave to cool, then spread into the flan case.
3 Core and thinly slice a red-skinned eating apple. Arrange the slices, overlapping so that the red skin shows, in a circle round the inside edge of the flan case.
4 Brush the slices with apricot glaze (see page 37). Bake in a moderately hot oven 375°F.—Mark 5, for 35 minutes.
5 Remove from the flan ring. Brush again with apricot glaze and leave until cold.

Quick Ways with Cakes and Pastries

All the basic recipes referred to in this chapter are listed in the Index.

1 Bake an oblong sandwich cake or sponge. Spread with apricot jam. Cover with a piece of almond paste (see page 37), rolled thinly. Press firmly on to the cake. Cut into fingers and decorate with halved cherries and diamonds of angelica.

2 Cut out rounds of sponge cake with a sharp 2-inch cutter. Pipe with vanilla flavoured butter cream (see page 33) and sprinkle with grated chocolate, or spread the top of each round with glacé icing (see page 34) and arrange chocolate buttons in a circle round the edge of each cake.

3 Drain one small can crushed pineapple. Stir into ½ pint thick custard and pour into a baked sponge flan case.

4 Drain a small can raspberries. Stir into an almost setting jelly that has been made with half a packet jelly and the juice from the can made up to ½ pint with water. Pour into a sponge or pastry case and decorate with cream if liked.

5 Sandwich two rounds of sponge cake with a thin layer of mincemeat and brandy or rum butter.

6 Roll small balls of rum or brandy butter in desiccated coconut. Place on hot apple or mincemeat tarts and serve at once.

7 Spread a cooked pastry flan case with raspberry jam. Crumble sponge cake over the jam to a depth of ½ inch. Moisten with sherry or fruit juice. Pour on cold, thick custard to fill the flan and, when set, decorate with cherries and angelica.

8 Cut small bananas in half and then lengthways. Brush with lemon juice and coat with cake crumbs or ground almonds. Cut fingers of sponge cake a little larger than the bananas. Spread each piece of cake with raspberry jam. Place a piece of banana on each and coat with melted chocolate.

9 Make cream buns with choux pastry. Fill with whipped cream mixed with canned strawberries or raspberries, well drained. Dust with icing sugar or coat the top of the bun with glacé icing (see page 34).

10 Cut a family size block of ice cream into 4 slices. Sandwich each between two thin slices Madeira or sponge cake, which have been spread with jam.

11 Line a pie plate with pastry. Cover with stewed sweetened fruit. Melt 3 oz. butter with 3 oz. syrup. Stir in 2 oz. quick cooking oats, 3 oz. desiccated coconut and 4 drops vanilla essence. Spread over the fruit and bake for 20 minutes in a hot oven.

12 Spread a flan case with raspberry jam. Cover with slices of banana tossed in lemon juice. Cover with whipped cream and sprinkle with grated chocolate.

13 Sandwich two oblongs of shortcrust pastry with mincemeat mixed with an equal quantity of marmalade. Seal the edges, brush with milk, sprinkle with sugar and bake in a hot oven for 20 minutes. Cut into slices when cold.

14 Sprinkle an open fruit tart thickly with coconut and brown sugar. Dot with butter and brown under a hot grill.

15 Quick frosting for a sponge cake—whisk an egg white until stiff. Whisk in 2 tablespoons melted red or blackcurrant jelly.

16 Spicy topping for a fruit cake or loaf—rub 1 oz. margarine into 2 oz. flour. Add 2 oz. sugar and a good pinch mixed spice. Sprinkle over the surface of the cake before baking.

17 Line pie dish with shortcrust pastry. Spread with mincemeat. Cover with a lattice made of strips of almond paste (see page 37) ½ inch wide. Bake in a hot oven for about 20 minutes.

18 Line a pie plate with shortcrust pastry. Cream 2 oz. butter with 2 oz. sugar. Beat in 1 egg, grated rind of 1 lemon, 1 oz. raisins, 1 oz. blanched chopped almonds, and 8 oz. grated cooking apple. Fill pastry case and bake in a moderate oven 30–40 minutes.

19 Line a deep 8-inch pie plate with shortcrust pastry. Bake blind for 10 minutes in a hot oven. Arrange drained, canned plums in the pastry case. Blend 2 egg yolks with a rounded tablespoon arrowroot. Stir in ½ pint plum juice and boil for 3 minutes, stirring. Add 1 oz. butter and leave to cool. Pour over the plums and top with meringue made with the egg whites. Bake in a slow oven for 30 minutes.

20 Line boat-shaped tins with flaky pastry, rolled thinly. Bake blind. Remove from the tin and leave until cold. Spread raspberry jam in the bottom of each. Fill with drained crushed pineapple. Pipe with cream and spike with toasted almonds.
Alternatively, spread cooked pastry boats with lemon curd and fill with drained mandarin oranges.

New Ways with Cakes and Pastries

Apricot layer cake

1 Sandwich two rounds of sponge cake with apricot jam and sliced drained apricots.
2 Cover with frosting which has been tinted apricot with a few drops of red and yellow colouring.
3 Decorate with blanched almonds and glacé cherries.

Chocolate peppermint cake

1 Bake two rounds of sponge or Victoria cake mix.
2 Cover the top of one round with chocolate peppermint creams.
3 Return to the oven for two minutes until the chocolate has melted.
4 Spread the softened chocolate over the surface of the cake, and sandwich the two rounds with chocolate butter cream.

Meringue layer cake

1 Bake two 8-inch rounds of sponge cake, and make two rounds of meringue the same size.
2 Arrange layers of sponge and meringue, sandwiching them with whipped cream and drained, canned fruit.

Quick party cake

1 Sandwich two rounds of sponge cake with butter cream flavoured with rum.

2 Coat cake with glacé icing, allow to set.
3 Melt 3 oz. chocolate; when cool, spoon over the top of the cake, allowing it to run down the sides.
4 Sprinkle with chopped almonds, if liked.

Pineapple cream cake

1 Stir 1 tablespoon crushed pineapple into a Victoria sandwich mixture.
2 Sandwich the cooked and cooled cake with whipped cream or butter cream to which the remaining pineapple has been added.
3 Coat with glacé icing, tinted yellow if liked.

Chestnut cream cake

1 Sandwich two rounds of cake, Victoria or sponge, with chestnut cream, made by mixing 8 oz. sieved chestnuts with ¼ pint whipped cream and sweetened with icing sugar.
2 Coat the cake with vanilla flavoured glacé icing.

Tea-party special

1 Sandwich two rounds of sponge cake with a creamy filling.
2 Brush the cake with warm apricot jam or glaze, coat with thinly rolled almond paste.
3 Pour thin glacé icing over, and sprinkle with chopped toasted almonds.

Lemon meringue cake

1 Bake a 9-inch sponge cake.
2 Spread top and sides with lemon curd.
3 Coat the edge with crushed meringue, and decorate the top with small, crisp meringues.

Lazy-daisy cake

1 Sandwich two rounds of sponge or sandwich cake with lemon flavoured butter cream.
2 Cover with frosting or icing.
3 Decorate with drained mandarin oranges, arrange in groups over the top of the cake to represent the petals of a flower, with a halved cherry in the centre of each.

Butter iced gâteau

1 Sandwich two rounds of cake with vanilla butter cream.
2 Coat the sides of the cake with butter cream and roll in chocolate vermicelli.
3 Spread butter cream over the top of the cake.
4 Decorate with halved walnuts.

Redcurrant tarts

1 Fill small cooked tartlet cases with cream cheese which has been blended with a little milk and sweetened to taste.
2 Spoon melted redcurrant jelly over the cheese and leave until set.

Fruit and custard tart

1 Stir $\frac{1}{4}$ oz. gelatine, dissolved, into $\frac{1}{2}$ pint sweetened fruit purée.
2 Pour into a cooked pastry case, leave until firm.
3 Cover with thick cool custard, and leave until set.

Banana tarts

1 Fill cooked pastry tartlet cases with confectioner's custard.
2 Toss sliced bananas in lemon juice, then arrange on top of the custard, and sprinkle with a little grated chocolate.

Pineapple almond tart

1 Line a pie plate with pastry, and bake blind in a hot oven.
2 When cold, cover with drained, crushed pineapple.
3 Make a lattice of thinly rolled almond paste and arrange over the pineapple.
4 Brush with egg and brown in a hot oven or under the grill.

Peach Melba tarts

1 Fill small cooked pastry cases with chopped peaches.
2 Cover with raspberry jelly which is on the point of setting.
3 Leave in a cool place until set.

Rhubarb and ginger meringue pie

1 Line a pie plate with pastry, bake blind.
2 When cold, fill with sweetened stewed or canned rhubarb, flavoured with a pinch of ginger.
3 Cover with meringue and bake for 30 minutes in a moderate oven.
4 Decorate with slices of preserved ginger, if liked.

Eve's tart

1 Line a pie plate with pastry.
2 Cover with sweetened stewed apple.
3 Top with Victoria sandwich mixture, made with 2 oz. flour, fat and sugar, and 1 egg.
4 Cook in a hot oven for about 30 minutes.

Banana custard flan

1 Dissolve 2 teaspoons gelatine in a little hot water, stir into $\frac{1}{2}$ pint warm custard.
2 When cool and almost set, stir in two or three sliced bananas.
3 Pour into a flan case, and sprinkle with coconut or grated chocolate, if liked.

Marshmallow fruit pie

1 Fill a baked pastry case with cooked or drained canned fruit.
2 Top with halved marshmallows.
3 Toast lightly under the grill for one or two minutes.

To serve cake as dessert

1 Place a round of sandwich cake 3–4 inches deep on a fireproof plate on a baking sheet.
2 Hollow out the centre, not quite through to the bottom.
3 Fill hollow with ice cream and drained cubes of pineapple.
4 Cover the whole cake with meringue (made with 4 oz. sugar and 2 egg whites), making certain that all the ice cream is sealed in.

5 Sprinkle with extra sugar.
6 Place in a very hot oven 450°F.—Mark 8, for 3–4 minutes until the meringue is flecked with gold.
7 Serve at once on the plate on which it was cooked.

Or:

Prepare as above, spreading hollow of cake with raspberry jam and filling with large cubes of frozen lemon mousse. Cover with meringue and finish in the same way.

Or:

Sandwich two squares or rectangles of sponge cake with slices of ice cream and drained canned or fresh soft fruit. Cover with meringue and finish as above.

Quick tips for Cakes and Pastries

To blanch almonds

1 Place whole almonds in a basin.
2 Pour boiling water over them and leave for about 5 minutes. Drain.
3 Pinch each nut between the thumb and finger, and the skin comes off easily.

To brown coconut

1 Place desiccated coconut in a shallow baking tin.
2 Brown gently in a warm oven.
3 When cool, place in an airtight jar to store.
4 Use for coating cakes.

To weigh syrup or treacle

1 Sprinkle the scale pan with flour before use, so that the syrup or treacle will slide from it.
2 Alternatively, weigh the tin of syrup. If using balance scales remove a weight equivalent to the amount of syrup required. Spoon syrup from the tin until the scales balance, e.g. if the tin of syrup weighs 1 lb. 12 oz. and 4 oz. is required, remove the 4 oz. weight from the scales.
3 If spring scales are used, spoon syrup from the tin until the dial shows 1 lb. 8 oz.

To chop nuts

1 Place the nuts in a neat pile in the centre of a chopping board.
2 Use a sharp knife with a long, straight blade. Move the handle and blade up and down, holding the point of the blade still.
3 Keep the nuts in a neat pile.

To cut angelica

1 If the angelica is hard, soak in hot water until pliable.
2 Drain and dry well.
3 Cut into narrow strips lengthways and then diagonally across each strip to make diamonds.

To make chocolate shapes

1 Melt chocolate in a bowl over a saucepan of hot water.
2 Spread thinly on a sheet of greaseproof paper laid on a flat surface.
3 Leave to set.
4 Cut into squares, triangles and diamonds, using a sharp knife with a long, straight blade. Alternatively, use small cutters to make fancy shapes.
5 The chocolate will peel from the paper.

To add colouring and flavouring

1 To ensure that just sufficient colouring or flavouring is added, dip the end of a skewer into the bottle and shake the liquid into the mixture, drop by drop.
2 Stir all the time, continuing to add more liquid until the mixture has the desired colour or flavour.

To make cream go further

1 When whipping double cream for piping or decorating add ¼ pint single cream to each ½ pint double cream, and whisk together.
2 Alternatively, whip ¼ pint double cream until thick and fold in two stiffly whisked egg whites, adding a little castor sugar if desired.
3 For pouring, use half double and half single cream. Whip together, adding a little castor sugar if desired.

To cream fat easily

1 When butter or margarine is hard, warm the mixing bowl by filling it with hot water.
2 Dry the bowl thoroughly.
3 Cut the fat into small pieces and put them into the bowl.
4 Heating the fat itself causes it to become oily.

To make an even layer cake

1 When making a sandwich or layer cake, weigh the cake tins filled with cake mixture.
2 Make sure that each weighs the same, so that each layer will be of even thickness.

To test that a sponge is cooked

1 Press the centre of the cake very lightly with the finger.
2 If cooked, it will spring back immediately.
3 The sides of the cake will shrink slightly from the tin when cooked.
4 Also, listen to the cake. If it is gently sizzling it is not quite done.

To roll a Swiss roll

1 Turn out the sponge on to a sheet of greaseproof paper dredged with castor sugar.
2 Quickly trim the edges with a sharp knife.
3 Roll up the cake with the greaseproof paper, and leave to cool.
4 Unroll, spread with filling, and roll up again.

To ice little cakes neatly

1 Mix glacé icing stiffer than usual.
2 Drop a teaspoon of icing from the tip of the spoon on to the centre of the cake.
3 Hold the cake in one hand and swirl the icing round with the underside of the bowl of the teaspoon.

To make small iced cakes

1 Make a slab of cake and, when cool, cut into shapes with a sharp knife.
2 Place them on a wire cooling rack over a tray.
3 Brush each shape with apricot glaze to prevent lifting crumbs with the icing.
4 Spoon icing over the cakes, easing it down the sides, if necessary, with the teaspoon.
5 Put the decoration in place before the icing has completely set.

To decorate a cake using butter cream

1 Cover the cake with butter cream.
2 Use the handle of a fork or spoon, or a round-bladed knife to make a pattern. The prongs of a fork will make a basket-work pattern.
3 To decorate the sides use a cake ruler. Hold the serrated edge against the cake and gently draw the ruler round the sides.

To coat the sides of a cake

1 Place chopped nuts, coconut or chocolate vermicelli on a sheet of greaseproof paper.
2 Coat the sides of the cake with butter cream, icing or apricot jam.
3 Holding the cake by the top and bottom, roll the sides in the decoration until evenly coated.

To make a jelly glaze for a flan or cake

1 Make up a jelly of a suitable flavour with half the recommended quantity of water.
2 When syrupy and almost set, spoon the jelly over the flan or cake.
3 If the jelly is too liquid it will make the pastry or sponge soggy.

To save time when making pastry

1 Rub together fat and flour, but use larger quantities than usual—say 1 lb. flour and 8 oz. fat.
2 Store in an airtight container in a refrigerator or a cool place. The mix will keep for about 3 weeks in a refrigerator, less in a larder.
3 When required, remove an appropriate quantity of the mix and add water as usual.

To prevent pastry stretching

1 Pastry often shrinks during cooking because it has been stretched earlier. After rolling out the pastry allow it to relax for a few minutes before use.
2 To lift, lay the rolling pin at one end of the pastry and roll the pin along lightly, rolling up the pastry with it. Lift the pin and unroll the pastry on to the flan ring or pie.

To prevent a flan case leaking

1 Line the flan ring with pastry, and brush with egg white. Bake blind.
2 During baking, the egg white forms a layer which will prevent a runny filling from making the pastry soggy, or from leaking through tiny cracks.

Index

G

T